D0073470

The Undergraduate Curriculum:
A Guide to Innovation and Reform

Other Titles in This Series

Teaching Strategies for the College Classroom, James R. Davis

A Handbook on Open Admissions, Anne F. Decker, Ruth Jody, and Felicia Brings

A College in Dispersion: Women at Bryn Mawr, 1896-1975, edited by Ann F. Miller

Planning for Higher Education: Background and Applications, Allan O. Pfnister

Going to College, James R. Davis

Freshman Seminar: A New Orientation, Robert D. Cohen and Ruth Jody

Westview Special Studies in Higher Education

The Undergraduate Curriculum:
A Guide to Innovation and Reform
Clifton F. Conrad

Recent pressures on undergraduate education have led to major--but often untutored--attempts to revitalize curricula. This comprehensive handbook is designed to aid faculty, administrators, and students engaged in curriculum reform at the undergraduate level. The emphasis throughout is on planning. Professor Conrad proposes a systems model for curriculum planning and examines four major areas: general and liberal education, area concentration, experiential learning, and calendar and degree programs. In each of these areas he identifies key issues, discusses the strengths and weaknesses of different approaches, provides a historical context, outlines major trends, and describes a variety of innovations that institutions might adopt. The result is a practical, usable book.

Clifton F. Conrad is associate professor of higher education at the College of William and Mary in Virginia; he previously taught at the University of Denver and Indiana University. Among his numerous publications are *Changing Practices in Undergraduate Education* and *The Implications of Federal Education Policy*.

The Undergraduate Curriculum:
A Guide to Innovation and Reform

Clifton F. Conrad

Westview Press / Boulder, Colorado

Westview Special Studies in Higher Education

Published in 1978 in the United States of America by
        Westview Press, Inc.
        5500 Central Avenue
        Boulder, Colorado 80301
        Frederick A. Praeger, Publisher

Library of Congress Catalog Card Number: 78-19637
ISBN: 0-89158-196-0

Printed and bound in the United States of America

Contents

Figures

Preface

The college and university curriculum has
received serious but uneven attention from writers
and scholars in the last several decades. In
general, writers on the subject take one of three
different approaches. One approach is to develop
a philosophical position, including statements
about what constitutes the essence of a good education. A second approach is to catalog and describe
a wide variety of curricular innovations, with
little regard for the differing philosophies they
may represent. A third approach is to develop
models and frameworks for curriculum planning.
While all of these approaches offer various advantages, few of these efforts are directed at the
professors, students, and administrators charged
with the task of curriculum planning. The main
purpose of this book is to help fill that gap by
proposing a framework for planning, while at the
same time identifying trends and innovations that
represent various approaches to undergraduate
education.

In this volume the term "innovation" refers to
any idea or practice perceived to be new by persons
in a large number of colleges and universities.
Thus, even if a specific curricular practice has
been around for decades, it is classified as innovative if it is generally perceived as being new.

The first two chapters provide a conceptual
framework for curriculum planning. In chapter one
the need for planning is discussed and three models
for analyzing the curriculum as an instructional
system are examined. The second and most important
chapter develops an alternative framework for
curriculum planning. The remaining four chapters
focus upon major trends and innovations in undergraduate education within four broad categories

of innovation. Chapter three discusses recent
developments in liberal and general education. In
the fourth chapter the focus is on concentration,
the various ways to develop what has traditionally
been called the "major." The fifth chapter
explores a wide range of innovations in experiential learning, while chapter six discusses changes
in the calendar and degree programs.

These last four chapters suggest a wide range
of innovations that institutions might consider in
planning their undergraduate program. Although the
format of presentation varies across the chapters,
the major focus of each chapter is on identifying,
discussing, and illustrating the various types of
innovations within each of the respective categories. A substantial part of the narrative is
devoted to illustrating the various approaches with
examples of practices implemented at selected
colleges and universities. In addition, the
strengths and weaknesses commonly associated with
different types of innovations are considered. To
provide needed context, each chapter also provides
some historical background and discusses some of
the key issues and controversies--all within the
general framework of "planning" for innovation.

In discussing examples of curricular innovation, I have taken the liberty of freely adapting
the descriptions found in college and university
catalogs and brochures without citing the source.
If a source seemed particularly important, I have
referred to individuals or materials. This procedure avoids the need for extensive direct quotation and citation, which would have placed a heavy
burden on the reader, while providing detailed
descriptions of many of these innovations. The
interested reader may wish to correspond directly
with institutions concerning information about
particular programs. Appendix A lists institutions
used in this study.

In addition to the many administrators and
faculty from across the country who have been
enthusiastic and generous in their support of this
project, several individuals deserve special mention: Jean Wyer Hatcher, Assistant Professor of
Business at the College of William and Mary, contributed in so many ways; in addition to assuming
major responsibility for chapter six, her substan-
tive and editorial comments are reflected throughout the book. Amy Worthington, a doctoral student
in higher education at the College of William and
Mary, assumed major responsibility for researching

innovations in experiential learning, contributing
substantially to the direction and content of
chapter five. Ellen Armstrong, Staff Associate,
Office of Student Services Policy Development at
Rutgers University, provided a thorough editing and
critique of the book.

James Davis, Director of the School of
Education at the University of Denver, made thoughtful comments on chapters one and two. Margaret
Wick, Dean of Briar Cliff College, was helpful in
providing insight into some of the key issues in
undergraduate concentration and made useful comments on an early draft of chapter four. My
colleague at the College of William and Mary,
Donald Herrmann, made useful comments on an early
draft and provided encouragement throughout the
project. Robert T. Blackburn, Professor of Higher
Education at the University of Michigan, first
introduced me to the study of curriculum and has
been a constant source of support throughout this
project.

Finally, I especially want to thank my wife,
Pam, for her continuing support. Her vitality,
enthusiasm, and unconditional support have enriched
immeasurably the quality of both my life and my
work.

July 1978   Clifton F. Conrad
Williamsburg, Virginia

1
The Curriculum as an
Instructional System

The diversity of American higher education may
nowhere be more evident than in the college and
university curriculum. In the past decade, the
proliferation of new learning experiences, programs,
and instructional methodologies has led many
observers to conclude that this has been one of the
most innovative periods in the history of American
higher education. A variety of explanations is
offered to account for recent curricular innovations, identifying several factors as major sources
of change: new types of students with different
needs and abilities, federal support for innovation
and reform, new ways of organizing knowledge, and
changing conceptions of learning and teaching. The
primary purpose of this book is to describe many of
these curricular changes and to propose a framework
that will be useful to professors and administrators involved in planning the undergraduate curriculum.

THE NEED FOR PLANNING: AN ILLUSTRATION

Confronted by various external and internal
pressures for change, postsecondary institutions
have reacted in various ways. In an unpublished
paper, Allan Pfnister (1971) identifies three
common approaches to curricular change. First,
many institutions avoid any semblance of planning
by using a "serendipity approach." That is, one or
more curricular innovations, such as changing the
college calendar or introducing a new career-
oriented major, are instituted without serious
attention to the relationship between the particular innovation and the existing academic program.
Changes are introduced one by one, without any

1

overall plan. Second, a "que sera, sera" approach is accepted: whatever will be, will be. Under this approach, institutions engage in little planning beyond recruiting good students, assembling an outstanding faculty, providing classrooms, and making library resources available. This approach also leads to the adoption of various curricular improvements without regard for the relationship between a proposed change and the existing curriculum. A third approach, which might be called a "systems approach," stresses careful planning of all aspects of the curriculum. Such an approach emphasizes the interrelation of all parts of the curriculum. Because the components of the program are interdependent, changes in one part of the system are likely to have implications for other parts. Accordingly, changes in the curriculum are made only in light of systemic curriculum planning. Conscious efforts are made to examine the relationships between the various elements of the curricular system and proposed changes.

The majority of institutions utilizes some combination of the first two approaches. Consequently, many promising innovations are, at best, only partly successful because of unintended results--pitfalls which might have been avoided through careful planning. To emphasize the need for planning within a "systems framework," it is useful to look closely at some unanticipated consequences of a curricular innovation introduced at one institution.

In the early 1970s, the University of Denver received a five-year grant from the National Endowment for the Humanities to establish an interdisciplinary program in the humanities. Altogether, nearly two million dollars had been raised when the program went into effect in the fall term of 1971. Students who elected the Humanities Block concentrated exclusively on the study of the humanities for a single quarter and earned fifteen quarter hours of credit. Interdisciplinary team-taught courses focused on particular cultural periods such as Classical Athens, Gothic Paris, Elizabethan England, and Gupta India.

When the program was implemented, it was widely heralded as an exciting new innovation in liberal education. While the program was ostensibly well-conceived, few persons were prepared for some of the unintended consequences. For example, during the first year of the program a number of issues were raised which involved participating faculty. What academic units would be responsible for paying the salaries of participating faculty? How should the "faculty load" be computed for team teaching? What should the qualifications of the faculty be? How should participating faculty be evaluated in terms of promotion, tenure, and salary increases?

Not surprisingly, a critical issue concerned the trend toward more students taking a greater proportion of their work in the humanities than in the natural and social sciences. During a period of declining enrollments at the University, other divisions reacted strongly to this development and its implications for attracting students to courses in their own departments.

There were also some unanticipated consequences for students taking the Humanities Block. For example, participation in the program might disturb a student's course sequence plan by forcing him to postpone a course that was a prerequisite to further work in an area of specialization. During the early stages of the program, students were given only one grade for the entire block; there was some risk involved for students in selecting this option.

From an administrative viewpoint, there was a host of related issues that emerged during the first year. Where should the program be located? Who should administer the program? How would the Humanities Block program affect the relationships between the schools and departments of the University? Put simply, some of the consequences of this new program were not anticipated and problems arose which posed serious questions about the future of the Humanities Block.

Although outside funding for the program has now expired, portions of the Humanities Block have thus far been maintained at the University. However, there is some debate surrounding the program, and its continuation is taking a different form. While the absence of outside funding may be chiefly responsible for this uncertainty, it is also probably true that more careful planning from the outset might have resulted in a greater degree of stability for the program by systematically integrating it with the entire curriculum. In any event, this example demonstrates that the curriculum is a "system" with interdependent parts. Because the introduction of new elements is likely to have many unintended consequences throughout the system, institutions contemplating changes in the curriculum should opt for systemic curriculum planning instead of a "serendipity" or "que sera, sera" approach.

It is an underlying thesis of this book that the undergraduate curriculum should and can be more than an aggregate of disparate courses and experiences; the curriculum is more than a collection of professorial predilections and preferences. Thus, the curriculum should be conceived and modified only through a systems approach to curriculum planning.

THREE MODELS FOR CURRICULUM PLANNING

Broadly defined, the curriculum is the total of educational experiences designed to foster learning. The word *curriculum* is derived from a root word meaning "race course." Students have freely transposed the original meaning in a phrase more descriptive of their perceptions of the curriculum: a "rat race!" For some students it is no more than that. There is some value in pondering the metaphor of "the race course," however. When horses run a race course, there is a designated track for them to follow. There is a beginning and an end. In contrast, open field running, as in a fox hunt, is a freer, less structured experience. The goal is to catch the fox, but there is no prescribed way to do so. A curriculum, therefore, at the very least, implies an ordered set of experiences with a beginning and an end and hopefully some cumulative impact.

What are some of the principles one might employ for organizing and planning these experiences? What factors need to be considered in all curriculum planning? In response to these and other related questions, a wide variety of frameworks and models has been developed by those interested in planning the undergraduate curriculum. Three of these approaches merit special consideration.

In Basic Principles of Curriculum and Instruction, Ralph Tyler (1950) offers a broad framework for considering the instructional programs of a school or college in terms of basic purposes, functions, and structures. His framework is built around four fundamental questions which must be answered in developing any curriculum and plan of instruction:

4

1. What educational purposes should the
    school seek to attain?
2. What educational experiences can be provided
    that are likely to attain these purposes?
3. How can these educational experiences be
    effectively organized?
4. How can we determine whether these pur-
    poses are being attained [pp. 1-2]?

Tyler does not attempt to answer these questions, because the answers will probably vary from
one level of education to another and from one
school to another. Instead, he focuses on different methods for studying these questions. Tyler
suggests that the critical step in establishing a
curriculum is deciding what purposes or objectives
should be established. These objectives must be
defined in terms of the specified behavior
involved. Once objectives are stated, they can
then be converted into a curriculum. Learning
experiences which are appropriate for attaining the
objectives must be selected initially and then
organized into courses or sequences of courses. In
turn, the most effective curricula are those that
are most successful in achieving their educational
objectives. There is little doubt that Ralph
Tyler's slim volume has influenced many of those
involved in curriculum planning. Even today, over
a quarter of a century after it was first published,
it is a useful guide--if only because of the critical issues it raises. Yet at the same time, the
book is not especially helpful in relating various
philosophies of education to concrete programs for
organizing and planning the undergraduate curriculum, for most of Tyler's examples are drawn from
elementary and secondary education.

More recently, Paul Dressel (1971, pp. 22-24)
has proposed a useful framework for curriculum
analysis and planning. Dressel's focus is on the
crucial factors involved in all curriculum planning
at the college level. Figure 1.1 illustrates
Dressel's conception of those critical factors.

FIGURE 1.1   PAUL DRESSEL'S CONTINUUMS AND
             ESSENTIAL ELEMENTS

<u>Four Continuums:</u>

1. Individual Student ----- Disciplines
        Personal development   Mastery of
                                   content
        Behavioral   Structure and
            orientation   methodology
                                   of disciplines
        Affective concerns   Scholarly
                                   objectivity

2. Problems, Policies,   Abstractions,
        Actions -------------   Ideas, Theories
        Competences   Verbal facility
        Present and future   Past oriented
            oriented

3. Flexibility, Autonomy -- Rigidity,
                                Conformity
        Adaptation to   Prescribed pro-
            individual's   gram and
            needs and   standards
            interests   based on
                                   demands of
                                   disciplines
                                   and/or
                                   "average"
                                   student or
                                   ideal scholar
        Democratic   Authoritarian

4. Integration,   Compartmentaliza-
        Coherence, and   tion, Inconsis-
        Unity in and from   tency, and
        Learning   Discord in
        Experiences ------   Learning
                                   Experiences

<u>Five Essential Elements:</u>

1. Liberal and vocational education
2. Breadth and depth
3. Continuity and sequence
4. Conception of learning and teaching
5. Continuing planning and evaluation

According to Dressel's model, institutions must make various judgments about what to emphasize. After selecting a desired position for the curriculum on the four continuums, planners must then consider five essential elements which are recurrent concerns in implementing a curriculum. Finally, although they are not shown in the figure, Dressel identifies a number of facilitating agents, such as requirements and grading systems, which "should give to a curriculum the character implied by choices of points along the continuums and of essential elements [Dressel, 1971, p. 29]."

Without describing Dressel's framework in detail, it is important to emphasize that Dressel has identified most, if not all, of the crucial factors involved in curriculum planning at the college level. His more or less neutral structure can be viewed as a useful tool for institutions involved in evaluating current programs or planning new ones.

Although Dressel has avoided the difficulties associated with Tyler's emphasis on ends, he has concentrated too exclusively on means. Thus, paradoxically, while Tyler may be guilty of placing too much emphasis on the importance of goals and objectives, Dressel may have gone too far in the opposite direction. Neither Tyler nor Dressel has built a sturdy bridge linking purposes and structures.

A third model for curriculum planning has been proposed by Joseph Axelrod. In a little-known but extremely useful paper, Axelrod (1968) presents a model for curriculum analysis that identifies six basic elements: three structural and three implemental. The former are the more formal aspects of the curriculum while the latter refer to the informal structure or sets of conditions under which the structural elements come to be realized. The three structural elements are content, schedule, and certification; the three implemental elements are group/person interaction, student experience, and freedom/control.

It is important to note that Axelrod has proposed a model that views the curricular-instructional process as a "system." As he states it (1968):

> Since the curricular-instructional process works as a system, we cannot change only one element in the system in any substantial way and expect the change to "take." There is a

certain reciprocity between each element in
the system and all of the other elements
(although each has a certain autonomy, too),
and before we can successfully reform one
aspect of the process we must understand pro-
foundly the connections between it and the
other elements in the system [p. 1].

As a consequence of this viewpoint, Axelrod suggests that an analysis based on the systems
approach forces the investigator to ask certain
questions about the connections between each of the
elements in the curricular-instructional subsystem
and all five of the others. Thus, Axelrod (1968,
p. 3) suggests that the investigator will initially
have to ask fifteen questions about these interrelationships as indicated in Figure 1.2.

FIGURE 1.2. THE FIFTEEN MAJOR QUESTIONS

--end ELEMENT	Interrelationships between ELEMENT					
	I CON- TENT	II SCHED- ULE	III CER- TIFI- CA- TION	IV IN- TER- AC- TION	V EXPE- RI- ENCE	VI FREE- DOM
I CONTENT		1	2	3	4	5
II SCHEDULE	1		6	7	8	9
III CERTIFICATION	2	6		10	11	12
IV INTERACTION	3	7	10		13	14
V EXPERIENCE	4	8	11	13		15
VI FREEDOM	5	9	12	14	15	

Axelrod has made an important contribution in establishing that the curriculum is a system, made up of various elements with a certain interrelationship and reciprocity. His framework sensitizes curriculum planners to the range of unintended consequences which may result from the introduction of a new program or element in the system. By implication, Axelrod emphasizes the importance of planning curricular changes with an eye toward the possible consequences for the entire system.

At the same time, Axelrod's framework is not detailed enough to be helpful in planning the undergraduate curriculum. Thus, while he may have gone beyond Tyler and Dressel in providing a more comprehensive analytic structure, he has also failed to provide the linkage between desired objectives and curricular structure. The next chapter outlines an alternative framework for planning the undergraduate curriculum.

REFERENCES

Axelrod, Joseph. "Curricular Change: A Model for Analysis." The Research Reporter, 3 (1968). University of California, Berkeley: Center for Research and Development in Higher Education.
Dressel, Paul L. College and University Curriculum. 2nd ed. Berkeley, California: McCutchan, 1971.
Pfnister, Allan O. "Curriculum Change: Chaos or Conspiracy." Unpublished paper, 1971.
Tyler, Ralph W. Basic Principles of Curriculum and Instruction. Chicago: University of Chicago Press, 1950.

2
Organizing Principles

Let us assume that a college or university is faced with the challenge of undertaking a comprehensive review of the undergraduate curriculum. We will also assume that there is some acceptance of the view that the curriculum operates as a system, whether we like it or not. Furthermore, we will assume that a rational approach to planning is possible, at least to some degree, and that the planning process is more than a political game, whereby department and divisional chairpersons work out agreements which express the self-interest of their various faculties. Granted these assumptions, is it possible to develop a framework for planning which is at once theoretical and specific?

A FRAMEWORK FOR PLANNING

Figure 2.1 suggests three major steps involved in planning the curriculum. The first and most important step involves the selection of an organizing principle on which to base the curriculum. As the figure indicates, five major organizing principles have been identified: academic disciplines, student development, great books and ideas, social problems, and selected competences. Let us examine each one briefly.

Perhaps unwittingly, the majority of postsecondary institutions organizes its curriculum around the academic disciplines. Since the organization of knowledge has taken place through self-contained disciplines, it is usually assumed that knowledge should be communicated in the same pattern. By force of tradition, this principle will probably continue as the basis of most curricular structures. However, in the last few decades, at least four

10

FIGURE 2.1. A FRAMEWORK FOR CURRICULUM PLANNING

Step 1: Choosing an Organizing Principle

   1. Academic Disciplines
   2. Student Development
   3. Great Books and Ideas
   4. Social Problems
   5. Selected Competences

Step 2: Establishing Curricular Emphases

   Four Continua:

   1. Locus of Learning:
         Campus-Based   Experiential
            Classroom Learning --   Learning

   2. Curriculum Content:
         Breadth --------------- Depth

   3. Design of Program:
         Faculty --- Contractual --- Student

   4. Flexibility of Program:
         Required -- Distribution -- Elective

Step 3: Building a Curricular Structure

   Some Considerations:

   1. Requirements for the total degree pro-
       gram, probably including general edu-
       cation, concentration, and electives.

   2. Alternative degree programs, including
       accelerated degree programs, external
       degree programs, and student-designed
       programs.

   3. Arrangements for concentration,
       including discipline-based majors,
       interdisciplinary majors, student-
       designed majors, and career-oriented
       majors.

   4. Components of general education,
       including core programs,

11

interdisciplinary programs, competence-
based programs, and freshman seminars.

5. Experiential learning opportunities,
including work-learning and service-
learning programs, cross-cultural
experiences, academic credit for
prior learning, and individual growth
experiences.

6. Calendar arrangements, including daily,
weekly, and annual schedules as well
as modular and interim arrangements.

7. Formal and informal structural arrangements for learning, ranging from the
traditional classroom to cluster
colleges and living-learning centers.

8. Individual course experiences, including the number and subject area of
courses to be offered.

9. Overall course structure, ranging from
structured classroom courses to
seminars and independent study.

10. Methods of student evaluation, ranging
from grades and comprehensive examinations to written evaluations and
external assessment.

11. Selection and advising of students.

12. Administrative and financial responsibilities for organizing and managing
the curriculum.

alternative ways of organizing the curriculum have gained a foothold in American higher education.

The curriculum can be organized so that its major goal is the facilitation of student development. A curriculum organized around this axis assumes that the development of the "whole person" is central to planning the undergraduate program. The main purpose of the curriculum is to promote both the affective and cognitive growth of students.

A third approach organizes the curriculum around great books and ideas. While persons favoring this approach do not necessarily downgrade the contributions of the academic disciplines or take issue with the goal of student development, they are in agreement that the major contributions in human thought can be captured in a selection of great books and great ideas--classics considered essential to Western civilization. Accordingly, they argue that the important issues facing mankind are timeless, and that the curriculum can best be structured around a series of carefully selected works.

The social problems approach is most concerned with the organization and communication of knowledge most needed to solve current problems. This approach is based on the premise that knowledge can best be communicated through a study of social problems--such as pollution, population control, and transportation--rather than through traditional disciplines or through the classics. It is both contemporary and futuristic in orientation, stressing the importance of the application of knowledge.

Finally, a major new way of organizing the undergraduate curriculum is to provide educational experiences that will enable students to develop selected competences. Emphasis is placed on the achievement of certain levels of competence such as the ability to read with high levels of comprehension, to write and speak fluently, and to use statistics and computers. Thus in contrast to the other approaches, which usually evaluate student performance only in terms of passage through a number of courses and the accumulation of credits, the selected competences approach places major emphasis on the identification of skills and abilities and on the process of assessing student progress toward the achievement of specific educational goals.

It should be emphasized that these organizing principles are not primarily distinguished from one another at a broad philosophical level. Persons favoring the academic disciplines or a great books

and ideas approach, for example, may have similar
educational philosophies. The crucial distinctions,
instead of residing at the philosophical level, lie
in the way knowledge is organized and communicated.
To the extent that institutions can find agreement
on one or more of these bases for planning, within
the broad context of overall institutional goals, a
solid foundation can be laid for building the curriculum.

After choosing an organizing principle, the
second step in curriculum planning is the selection
of emphases. Figure 2.1 exhibits four continua
which curriculum planners need to consider. The
first continuum refers to the locus of learning by
comparing campus-based classroom learning with
experiential learning. Historically, college and
university curricula have favored one end of the
continuum: traditional classroom learning. In
recent years, however, many institutions have moved
closer to the middle of the continuum by offering a
variety of experiential learning opportunities.
(Chapter five discusses a number of these experiential learning programs such as work-learning and
service-learning programs.)

The second continuum refers to the content of
the curriculum and compares *breadth* and *depth*. For
our purposes, breadth refers to a basic knowledge
of some of the essential facts and concepts in all
major areas of knowledge and, in addition, some
understanding of the structure, concepts, and
modes of thought utilized in academic inquiry.
Accordingly, breadth is achieved through the use of
various modes of knowing to illustrate the foundations as well as the substance of the major areas
of knowledge. While most curricula emphasize
breadth through the general education program, it
can also be achieved through the manner in which a
subject is introduced. For example, a course in a
student's major may emphasize breadth because the
subject is placed within the context of a larger
body of knowledge.

The concept of depth can be an even more difficult term, usually referring to study in a field
of concentration. For our purposes, depth will be
defined as a detailed knowledge of the concepts,
terminology, and methodology of a particular way of
organizing knowledge--such as through the academic
disciplines. Although study in breadth and study
in depth may seem mutually exclusive, they are but
two points on a continuum and can complement one
another. The critical issue is the relative weight

14

given to study across various fields of knowledge (breadth) versus the intensive study of a particular approach to organizing and communicating knowledge (depth). Most institutions fall somewhere in the middle on this continuum, but as we shall see in chapter three, there is some evidence that breadth may have been receiving less emphasis in the last several years through the reduction of general education requirements.

The third continuum refers to the design of the program; that is, whether the program is faculty-designed, student-designed or is a contract between faculty and student. In most institutions, of course, faculty retain complete control over the design of a student's program, usually through a broad set of requirements agreed upon by the faculty as a whole. In recent years, as students have demanded a greater share in planning their own programs, there has been a marked shift in a number of institutions moving toward the midpoint on the continuum. Usually this position on the continuum is represented by a contract where the student more or less designs his own program, subject only to faculty approval. While a totally student-designed program is conceivable, only a handful of institutions surrenders to students the final approval over their plan of study. The distinction between faculty designed and contractually-designed programs is an important one, with many students today playing an important role in the design and evaluation of their academic program.

The last continuum refers to the flexibility of the program and compares a highly structured or required program to a wide-open or elective program. The issue here is not who designs the content, but what is required. There are three distinct types of courses, or sets of experiences, that can be represented on this continuum. Required courses are defined as those specific courses and experiences that students must present for graduation; distribution courses are defined as those within a content division, department, or group, where some freedom of choice is allowed the student; elective courses are those which can be taken from among the listing of courses of the institution without any restrictions, except the meeting of prerequisites. In practice most institutions offer all three types of courses, but many schools choose to emphasize one end of the continuum or the other.

The establishment of curricular emphases should not be viewed as a needless exercise.

Indeed, the conscious selection of various points on the continua will have important implications for the expression of the organizing principles.

Only after the curricular emphases have been wedded to one or more of the organizing principles should attention be turned to the building of a curricular structure. This third step in curriculum planning involves the translation of these principles and emphases into an integrated curriculum plan. Figure 2.1 lists the various tasks which must be undertaken to develop the curriculum into a fully elaborated undergraduate program. Unfortunately, most curriculum planning begins with Step 3 rather than Steps 1 and 2.

This framework for curriculum development can be used in a variety of ways. It can serve as a tool for analyzing a total institutional curriculum or parts of the undergraduate program such as general education, the major, and various special programs. In addition, it can serve as a device for analyzing new curricular innovations. It also provides a stimulus for imagining new curricular arrangements based upon alternative combinations of organizing principles and emphases. Most important, it can serve as a tool for planning all or part of the undergraduate program. By forcing curriculum planners to think in terms of organizing principles and curricular emphases, it encourages the construction of a curriculum that reflects a systematic approach to the undergraduate program instead of a hodgepodge of unrelated courses and experiences. With those goals in mind, the underlying purpose of this volume is to develop and demonstrate the model so that it can be easily utilized by those involved in curriculum planning.

In order to expand upon the framework, it is necessary to develop in detail the five organizing principles. For each of the latter, I will look at the background and basic premises of the approach and the combinations of curricular emphases that are often associated with that organizing principle. An example of how one or more institutions have organized their curricula around each principle will be presented. Finally, some strengths and weaknesses associated with each principle will be considered.

THE ACADEMIC DISCIPLINES AS AN ORGANIZING PRINCIPLE

It has long been argued that the way in which

the curriculum is formulated depends on the way in
which the structure of knowledge is conceived.
Central to this issue are at least three questions
that have concerned philosophers for centuries: How
do we define knowledge? How do we "get" knowledge? How do we verify what is or is not knowledge? Beginning with fundamental Platonic and
Aristotelian differences over the definition of
knowledge and how knowledge can be verified, philosophers such as Locke, Hume, Berkeley, and Kant
have addressed these critical issues.

The purpose here is only to raise these epistemological issues, for a primary concern of this
analysis is the ways in which man has organized
knowledge for academic study, particularly through
the academic disciplines. Before discussing the
academic disciplines as an organizing principle,
we might ask: What are some of the other ways in
which man has organized knowledge in recent times?
John Dewey developed ten categories which have
served as the primary tool for organizing college
and university libraries. They have been super-
seded recently by the classification system of the
Library of Congress with its thirty-one basic categories. Mortimer Adler developed an organizing
tool for the Encyclopedia Britannica which also
uses ten categories, although they are different
from those of Dewey. Some conception of the structure of knowledge is consciously or unconsciously
employed in defining the nature and extent of the
curriculum. But which of the different conceptions
of the structure of knowledge, if any, should provide a unifying principle for the curriculum?

One response to that question is the academic
disciplines. From an historical viewpoint, the
organization of the disciplines is a recurring
issue. Aristotle, for example, delineated three
classes of disciplines: the theoretical disciplines
(such as metaphysics, mathematics, and the natural
sciences), the practical disciplines (such as
ethics and politics), and the productive disciplines (such as fine arts, the applied arts, and
engineering). Other well-known schemes have been
put forward by such diverse persons as Plato,
Auguste Comte, and, more recently, Philip Phenix.
Each of these schemes has at various times influenced the organization and definition of the
disciplines.

A number of definitions of the term
"discipline" have been suggested. For our purposes, the definition developed by Arthur King and

17

John Brownell is most useful. They suggest that a discipline is: a community of persons; an expression of human imagination; a domain; a tradition; a syntactical structure--a mode of inquiry; a conceptual structure; a specialized language or other system of symbols; a heritage of literature and artifacts and a network of communications; a valuative and affective stance; and an instructive community (King and Brownell, 1966, p. 95).

The organization of the disciplines within higher educational institutions has always been subject to change. The history of curriculum development in the American college and university illustrates the changes that have taken place in the organization of the disciplines. Neither the number nor the structure of acceptable disciplines for college and university studies has ever been static. New disciplines have emerged, providing the basis for new traditions. Many of the contemporary social and natural science disciplines were gradually included within the curriculum in the late nineteenth and early twentieth century and only after considerable controversy. The concomitant growth of the academic department has further led to the strengthening of various disciplines.

Persons espousing the academic disciplines as a major organizing principle suggest that the curriculum should reflect the existing state of knowledge as defined through the departmental and disciplinary structure. Put simply, the curriculum should be structured around the academic disciplines. King and Brownell, among others, suggest that the major way of organizing and communicating knowledge is through an acquaintance with the concepts and modes of inquiry provided by the disciplines (King and Brownell, 1966, pp. 146-149).

While the structure and organization of knowledge have not remained static, the American undergraduate curriculum today reflects the dominance of well-established academic disciplines and departments. Indeed, the organizational structure of most colleges and universities, by perpetuating the authority of academic departments, is a powerful force for maintaining the status quo in curricular organization.

Applying this organizing principle to the framework for curriculum planning, it can be seen that several emphases (refer to Step 2 of Figure 2.1) are often associated with a discipline-based approach. For obvious reasons, the locus of learning is almost invariably campus-based--in the

18

classroom--with few, if any, provisions for experiential learning. The content may emphasize breadth through the general education program, but is also likely to emphasize depth to the extent that general education is based upon courses in particular disciplines. The concentration portion of a student's program usually represents depth by definition, and even the elective portion is likely to be based in a few disciplines. The design of the program will likely reflect faculty control, although its flexibility may range from highly prescriptive or required to elective courses. These trends on the various continua notwithstanding, there is considerable variation in the curricular structures (refer to Step 3) that are utilized by postsecondary institutions.

Because the majority of undergraduate curricula is based on this organizing principle, it is unnecessary to provide an institutional example of a discipline-based curriculum. It is more appropriate to identify some of the possible strengths and weaknesses of such an approach to organizing the undergraduate program.

A number of advantages to organizing the academic program around the disciplines have been noted. Perhaps the most compelling argument is that knowledge in the modern world is principally organized around the disciplines and can thus best be understood and communicated through the disciplines. As Philip Phenix (1964) states it:

> The most impressive claim the disciplines have upon the education is that they are the outcome of learning that has actually been successful. A discipline is a field of inquiry in which learning has been achieved in an unusually productive way. Most human efforts at understanding fail. A very few succeed, and these fruitful ways of thought are conserved and developed in the disciplines. Every discipline is simply a pattern of investigation that has proved to be a fertile field for the growth of understanding [p. 36].

Put simply, one major advantage is that this approach is based on a widely accepted epistemology, namely that the disciplines are the single best way of organizing and communicating knowledge.

There are also a number of practical advantages in planning the undergraduate program around the academic disciplines. Since most colleges and

19

universities are organized by academic departments
based on the various disciplines, it is administra-
tively efficient to organize the curriculum around
the department rather than another organizing principle which cuts across the existing academic
organization. Also, since the majority of postsecondary institutions rely on the disciplines as the
basis of curricular formation, a similar curriculum
allows students to transfer easily from one institution to another.

Although most planners would agree that the
curriculum should impart to the student some understanding of the disciplines, many persons raise
serious questions about the hegemony enjoyed by
discipline-based programs. Some people have
attacked the very classification of knowledge by
academic discipline, pointing out that there are a
number of sound alternative schemes which offer
distinct advantages. Still others suggest that
given the development of so many disciplines it is
difficult, if not impossible, to structure the curriculum in a way that incorporates the major concepts and modes of inquiry common to the disciplines.

While the epistemological issues will likely
remain unresolved, a more concrete criticism is
that even if the structure of knowledge should be
based on disciplines, the structure of the curriculum should still be based on educational goals and
designated learning experiences. Robert Pace (1966)
observes:

> In higher education today knowledge is orga-
> nized around academic disciplines. This orga-
> nization has a special relevance for scholars
> and researchers and it is certainly not irrel-
> evant for the ordinary student. It is never-
> theless a clerical organization of knowledge
> which serves most directly the interests of
> the academic priesthood . . . [pp. 39-40].

Many persons today share Pace's concern with
the dominance of the academic discipline. Some go
a step further, however, and argue that alternatives
to the narrow, knowledge-consumption view reflected
in the disciplinary approach call for other organizing principles such as student development or
competence-based curricula. In particular, a
discipline-based curriculum may indicate a lack of
concern for the affective development of students
as well as for their individually preferred

20

educational goals.

Oddly enough, some of the strongest criticisms of the disciplinary approach are coming from within the disciplines themselves. The rigid boundaries and specialized language of the disciplines hamper both the application of knowledge to contemporary problems and the extension of basic research. The biologist today must know what the chemist and physicist are talking about to carry on more penetrating investigations within the field of biology. Furthermore, all three must be able to talk to political scientists and sociologists if what they have discovered is ever going to "do the world any good." Requests for mechanisms for carrying on the interdisciplinary studies often come from the most advanced and specialized scholars within the disciplines.

While the academic disciplines are likely to continue to dominate the structure of undergraduate curricula, attention is being given to other organizing principles.

STUDENT DEVELOPMENT AS AN ORGANIZING PRINCIPLE

There have always been proponents of the view that the proper foundation for curriculum planning should be the development of students as persons. In the early years of the Republic, this viewpoint was often referred to as the "character building" conception of the college. In spite of its widespread acceptance, this organizing principle has not historically provided the underpinnings of many college and university curricula.

In the last several decades, however, there has been a "developmental" movement that has attracted widespread attention and has led, in a number of institutions, to the adoption of a curriculum based upon some conception of students' developmental needs. The modern roots of this approach can be traced to the work of such developmental psychologists as Nevitt Sanford and Joseph Katz.

Attacking the grip of the professions or disciplines, Sanford and Katz view the development of personality as the prime meaning of undergraduate liberal education (Sanford and Katz, 1962, p. 424). Their main argument is that in planning the curriculum, educators should

. . . ignore conceptions of what college students "ought to know," whether the concern be

21

with their preparation for more advanced
courses or with a suitable sampling of organized knowledge, and that we ought to concentrate instead on giving these students
experiences that set in motion the developmental changes in which we are interested
[p. 434].

Operating out of a Freudian developmental
framework, Sanford and Katz offer some general
guidelines for organizing the curriculum around
student developmental needs--such as allowing the
entering student freedom to indulge in those interests that he already has and teaching subjects in a
way that addresses the student's existential concerns. More recently, other developmentalists,
such as Arthur Chickering and Kenneth Keniston,
have charted the stages and tasks which most undergraduates must confront.

While there are often major differences among
developmentalists regarding the particular definition of the developmental tasks facing adolescents
and young adults during their college years, the
developmentalists are united by their basic
approach. Most important, they usually agree that
the curriculum should not be organized around preparing people to enact social roles, but around
helping students "put themselves together
internally," that is, encouraging developmental
growth. They also see a need for the integration
of emotion and feeling with intellectual and cognitive growth. College should be a place and time
for students to have a psycho-social moratorium
from making decisions, so that they can find out
who they are and where they are going.

Arthur Chickering integrates much of the developmental literature by demonstrating how college
can make a difference along seven major vectors of
change: developing competence, managing emotions,
developing autonomy, establishing identity, freeing
interpersonal relationships, finding purpose, and
developing integrity (Chickering, 1969, pp. 9-19).
Not only does Chickering identify the commonalities
in the developmental tradition, he also draws upon
the existing literature to try to identify the
institutional conditions that make a difference to
student development. With regard to the curriculum,
Chickering (1969) suggests:

The principal curricular change would be
increased flexibility. Increased flexibility

22

could be achieved by adding opportunities for
independent study and for groups of students
to work together with an instructor in a large
and amorphous area--which could take more def-
inite shape as these students defined more
clearly their own interests and as the significant components of the area itself became
known. Flexibility could be enhanced by opportunities to put together courses from diverse
domains, or to pursue fewer courses more
exhaustively. Time units might also be loos-
ened. Some students and faculty members might
develop an area for study and then fit the
time to the study--putting the horse before
the cart, in proper fashion for a change--
rather than the other way around, where a
fixed time unit is set and all subjects cut to
fit it [pp. 285-286].

Although Chickering's Education and Identity
is viewed as a classic by many espousing a developmental perspective, there are a number of other
sources. The Student in Higher Education (1968),
for example, a volume representing the Report of
the Committee on the Student in Higher Education,
includes some general recommendations regarding the
curriculum.
    To summarize briefly, proponents of this
approach are united by a conviction that the curriculum should be organized around student developmental growth. The curriculum should not be viewed
as an aggregate of discipline-based courses, but
rather as a flexible set of experiences designed
with the students' developmental growth as the
guiding principle.
    Applying this organizing principle to the
framework for curriculum planning, it can be seen
that several curricular emphases on the four continua (refer to Step 2) are often associated with
this approach, and further, that most of these
emphases tend toward the ends of the continua
opposite to the academic disciplines. The third
and fourth continua are particularly critical in
clarifying this approach. Significantly, the
developmentalists argue that a student's program
should be individually designed, usually through a
contract with the faculty. Student growth and curricular flexibility, in terms of the design of the
program, are viewed as inseparable by the developmentalists. It generally follows that the program
should also be highly flexible through an emphasis

23

in the major program on elective courses. Also
following from the notion of curricular flexibility
and student-designed programs, most developmentalists would argue that the locus of learning should
not be confined to campus-based activities; provisions should be made for off-campus experiential
learning. Finally, with regard to curriculum content, the developmental viewpoint seems to emphasize neither breadth nor depth, although many
programs tend initially to steer students in the
direction of breadth.

An interesting example of a curriculum conceived to facilitate developmental growth is the
Goddard College undergraduate program. In explaining the "Goddard idea," this excerpt from the
college catalog suggests the developmental focus of
the curriculum:

The Goddard idea about education is offered as
a reasonable basis for seeking answers, not as
an answer in itself.

The idea is that learning takes place as
persons discover their needs and move to meet
them.

Need-meeting experiences can give an individual a growing body of resources to draw on
in identifying and meeting new needs. They
may also be of such a nature as to make clear
the value of earlier experiences.

A learning experience is so defined here:
it is vital to the student's present needs,
illuminating of his past experience, and useful as a resource in his future life.

Such experience, it must be added, is in
the nature of a transaction. The learner
takes from her environment what will be useful
in meeting her needs--information, skills she
may observe and practice, advice, instruction--
and gives back to her environment a newly
modified, developing, and growing behavior
which becomes, in turn, part of the environment of resources for other learners. So this
transactional learning is social as well as
personal: many of the needs each individual
must meet derive from the human fact that she
is interdependent with others; and her behavior sums with the behaviors of millions of
other persons to become society, cultures,
civilizations, the human world [Goddard
College: The Resident Undergraduate Program,
1975-1976, pp. 9-10].

The curriculum at Goddard emphasizes flexibility, a contract-designed program, and a diverse offering of courses and experiences. Within guidelines established by the faculty, each student plans his own educational program, including at least two nonresident semesters.

At Goddard "curriculum" is defined as the whole life of the student, with particular emphasis not only on formal study activities but also on the student's ability to live cooperatively in a college residence, on performance in a college work program, and on participation in college governance. There are six main kinds of formal study activities: 1) group courses, which generally meet as discussion groups; 2) independent studies, which are planned by individual students with faculty who help them find resources and evaluate their work; 3) studio and workshop activities, in which the emphasis is on practical work with the assistance of faculty; 4) off-campus field-service work, in which students learn through serving in hospitals, schools, social agencies, and elsewhere in the community; 5) nonresident term studies, which usually involve apprenticeships, internships, or short-term enrollment in other educational institutions or programs under sponsorship of the college and faculty; 6) special summer sessions at Goddard, where a student devotes twelve weeks to working on a single issue or topic chosen from a limited number of offerings. A typical program for a student in a resident semester includes three study activities. Students are counselled to choose group courses during the first year, although they may include studio work and field-service experience. Additional study activities are utilized as the student moves through the program.

At the end of each term, a Goddard student writes evaluative reports about each activity. Reports are also written by a student's teachers, nonresident-term supervisors, counsellors, and others who share responsibility for the program. These reports become the basic materials for the periodic reviews that faculty members make of each student. Four such reviews take place during a student's eight terms at Goddard.

The first two years of the program are viewed as exploratory study. While Goddard has no "majors" in the traditional sense, at the end of the second year each student is asked to define her interests in an application for degree candidacy. With the assistance of a counsellor and other

25

faculty members, the student outlines the proposed area of study she wishes to make the core of studies during the last two years at Goddard. Usually in the next-to-last term, a candidate for the degree chooses a Senior Study committee made up of at least three faculty members, one of whom is her advisor. With the help of the committee, the student plans her Senior Study in considerable detail. As the Study nears completion, a final review focuses on the student's execution of the Senior Study plan against the background of her entire Goddard education. If the student's plan is carried out to the satisfaction of the committee and the document or product resulting from the Study meets the approval of committee members (and an additional person appointed by the Dean's office), the student will be graduated. The description of the various stages in a student's progress through Goddard suggests the importance attached to thorough evaluative reports written by students and their teachers. Goddard does not use letter or number grades; the reports are the sole basis for the preparation of transcripts of Goddard study.

The academic program at Goddard College is one example of organizing the undergraduate curriculum around student developmental needs. From its philosophical statements to the practical implementation of the curriculum--including a wide variety of nonconventional learning opportunities--the Goddard program represents a concrete alternative to many existing curricular arrangements.

The Goddard example suggests some of the potential advantages of organizing the curriculum around student development. The curriculum structure is likely to be highly flexible, thereby promoting the creativity of students and enhancing their motivation. Most of all, its proponents argue that such a curriculum will encourage colleges to once again nurture the "whole person." Regardless of whether or not one subscribes to this organizing principle, the overall contributions of the developmental movement in the last decade have been widely heralded. The movement has fostered the trend toward stripping away the last vestiges of *in loco parentis,* by encouraging greater freedom of choice and making students assume responsibility for planning their educational program.

While many persons acknowledge these contributions, some are quick to point out some of the potential deficiencies in this approach. Perhaps the most biting criticism is that it places insufficient attention on the acquisition of knowledge. As a consequence, it is myopic and overlooks a fundamental mission of the college and university: the transmission of knowledge. Charges of elitism are also leveled at this approach. Is college the appropriate institution for promoting development? Or is this a psychological luxury for privileged students? Should we encourage the "new students" in higher education (especially the disadvantaged) to be interested in personal development at the expense of preparing for a career?

Other criticisms focus more directly on the application of a developmental framework for planning the curriculum. For example, some argue that students need more guidance than freedom, and a developmental approach clearly emphasizes the latter. Some are simply critical of any developmental framework, while others, who are perhaps more sympathetic, admit that there is little agreement regarding the particular developmental needs of college students; it is difficult to design a program without substantial agreement on those needs, however. In spite of these criticisms, some of which are met in the Goddard program, curricular formation based on student developmental needs is one alternative for organizing the curriculum.

GREAT BOOKS AND IDEAS AS AN ORGANIZING PRINCIPLE

Among those most deeply committed to the liberal arts, there has long been a disdain for many of the developments in the American undergraduate curriculum. From this viewpoint the elective system is often seen as a device which led to the multiplication of subject matters, the effect of which was hardly alleviated by the introduction of majors. The curriculum, through the dominance of the academic disciplines, has often been conceived in reference to the requirements of graduate and professional schools or to changing conditions of employment in the contemporary world, rather than to the pursuit of knowledge for its own sake. In short, liberal education has been undermined as the college curriculum has become fanatically preparatory.

In the past four decades, one attempt to recover the true meaning of the liberal arts has involved a new approach to the vast tradition of Western thought as embodied in the "great books."

Proponents of this approach argue that the wisdom of the past is distilled in selected great books which have come to be known as classics. Although our knowledge of the world is always expanding, the important problems confronting man and man's responses to them are those which have been dealt with by the great minds through the ages. While the form of the central problems confronting mankind may change, the substance of the problems will not. Thus, the content of the great books should be the foundation of learning.

This approach most emphatically rejects the domination of undergraduate education by the academic disciplines and the concomitant emphasis on specialization at the undergraduate level. Because the disciplines depend completely on a detailed understanding of the particular, attention is confined to a special subject matter. Discipline-based learning entails a fragmentation of the students' attention, a multiplication of special problems, instead of addressing the perennial problems of mankind--the hallmark of a liberal education.

The most ardent defenders of the great books call for the organization of the entire curriculum around selected classics. Academic departments, with their disciplinary base, should assuredly not occupy a position in the academic organization of a college committed to the great books approach.

Applying this organizing principle to the framework for analyzing curricular emphases, it is obvious that this approach stresses the left end of each of the four continua. Learning should principally occur in a classroom setting through the serious consideration of the great books; experiential learning, which is rooted in the present, is an anomaly to an approach that emphasizes the past. By implicitly denouncing the emphasis placed on discipline-based curricula, this approach almost exclusively emphasizes breadth in the content of the program. The faculty, who are obviously better prepared than students to select the great books, assume total responsibility for the design of the program. It follows that the program will probably be highly rigid, with at best only a few electives.

St. John's College, which began its great books program in 1937, is the only institution which has applied this principle to the organization of the entire academic program. The examination of a program which has survived and prospered for four decades provides some interesting insights into the development of a great books curriculum.

The College's organizing principle is explained in its catalog:

> St. John's College believes that the way to
> liberal education lies through the books in
> which the greatest minds of our civilization--
> the great teachers--have expressed themselves.
> These books are both timeless and timely; they
> not only illuminate the persisting questions
> of human existence, but also have great rele-
> vance to the contemporary problems with which
> we have to deal. They can therefore enter
> directly into our everyday lives. Their
> authors can speak to us almost as freshly as
> when they spoke for the first time, for what
> they have to tell us is not something of
> merely academic concern, remote from our real
> interests. They change our minds, move our
> hearts, and touch our spirits.
> The books speak to us in more than one way.
> In raising the persisting human questions,
> they lend themselves to different interpreta-
> tions that reveal a variety of independent and
> yet complementary meanings. And, while seek-
> ing the truth, they please us as works of art
> with a clarity and a beauty that reflect their
> intrinsic intelligibility. They are therefore
> properly called great, whether they are epic
> poems or political treatises, and whether
> their subject matter is scientific, historical,
> or philosophical. They are also linked
> together, for each of them is introduced, sup-
> ported, or criticized by others. In a real
> sense they converse with each other, and they
> draw each reader to take part, within the
> limits of his ability, in their large and
> unending conversation [St. John's College
> Catalog, 1976-1977, p. 5].

Although the list of books may vary slightly
from year to year, all students take the same
required program of great books--classics from
Plato and Aristophanes to Marx and Freud. There is
no departmental structure, and all faculty are
simply referred to as tutors. Except for preceptorials (nine week in-depth studies), there are no
electives.

There are three principal curricular vehicles
for the implementation of the St. John's program:
seminars, tutorials, and preceptorials. Students
attend seminars based on the great books for each

29

of the four years. Two tutors meet twice weekly
for several hours with fifteen to twenty students.
The seminar begins with a question asked by one of
the tutors, and thereafter consists almost entirely
of student discussion. The course of the session
is not fixed in advance; it is determined by the
process of discussing, of facing the crucial issues,
or of seeking bases upon which a line of reasoning
can be pursued.

The conversational methods of the seminar are
carried over into the tutorials. For four years a
student attends one language tutorial and one mathematics tutorial, usually four mornings a week.
Three times a week sophomores also attend a music
tutorial. As in the seminar, students talk freely
with one another and the tutor, but the discussion
focuses on assigned tasks. In addition, there are
four years of laboratory science. Groups of students meet with a tutor twice a week for science
laboratory to study such topics as theory of
measurement and atomic structure.

Preceptorials were added to the program in
1962. For roughly nine weeks in the middle of the
year the seminars of the junior and senior classes
are replaced by preceptorials. These are small
groups of students engaged in the study of one book
or the exploration of one subject in several books.
Although many preceptorials study one of the books
on the seminar lists, or a theme suggested by the
seminar reading, some preceptorials may deal with
books and themes the students would not otherwise
encounter in the program. The preceptorial is the
only part of the curriculum which offers the student some choice, since he may choose from among
the fifteen or twenty topics offered each year.
One additional component of the program is the
weekly formal lecture presented by an outside
tutor. The lecture is followed by a discussion
with both faculty and students participating.

In their study of undergraduate education,
Arthur Levine and John Weingart conducted a number
of interviews with students and faculty at St.
John's College. They concluded that in spite of
several drawbacks associated with the current organization of the program, there was widespread
approval of the overall thrust of the great books
program (Levine and Weingart, 1973, p. 48). In a
broader context, however, what are some of the
possible strengths and weaknesses of a program
based on the great books?

On the plus side, a great books program may

represent one of the most integrated courses of study offered in the entire nation. While using the great books as the principal vehicle for promoting the liberal arts, such a program can provide a firm foundation for further advanced study. Contrasted with the potpourri of disparate courses and experiences that characterizes most undergraduate programs, such a program may be highly appealing to those most committed to a vision of true liberal learning. While no institution other than St. John's has chosen to base its entire program on the great books, the attractiveness of this approach has led many educational reformers to devote part of their curriculum, especially in the general education program, to selected classic books in the history of Western civilization.

Yet the absence of support for the great books as an organizing principle for the entire curriculum suggests that there are some disadvantages. Foremost among them is the failure of the study of classical volumes to include new developments, a serious deficiency given the speed of knowledge expansion. Especially in the sciences it is argued, the increase in knowledge during the last twenty years has contributed more than in the entire previous history of mankind. A second criticism is that the program is primarily oriented toward the past rather than the present and the future. A third notes that at St. John's, the program tends to favor the humanities over the sciences and focuses exclusively on Western civilization, ignoring the intellectual contributions of the non-Western world. Also, it has been observed that such a program is necessarily rigid, allowing the student little choice to pursue his own interests. Finally, some persons suggest that while the concept may be attractive, it is impractical; students pay a price in terms of immediate job prospects and perceived readiness to engage directly in graduate work, because the majority of institutions focus on the preparation of students for graduate school and preprofessional training.

Regardless of whether or not one favors a great books approach, it deserves serious consideration, for in presenting an alternative to discipline-based curricula it raises some important issues regarding the more traditional academic program.

SOCIAL PROBLEMS AS AN ORGANIZING PRINCIPLE

Since education is largely a function of society, increasingly paid for by society, the focus of
collegiate education, it is sometimes argued, ought
to be on societal problems. The most pressing
problems today are social problems; without their
resolution, individuals, however gifted and tal-
ented, will not be able to develop to their full-
est. This point of view has led to a new basis
for planning the curriculum, a social problems
approach.

A curriculum utilizing this approach is
broadly organized around one or more themes such as
environmental problems, urban problems, or world
order. Most of these programs are characterized by
a problem orientation, a concern for social responsibility, and a belief in the need to integrate
knowledge. Several distinctive program emphases
have generally evolved from these principles:
flexibility and student initiative in curriculum
development, an orientation toward emphasizing the
present and future instead of the past, and off-
campus learning through community action and practical experience. In utilizing a social problems
approach, institutions do not usually organize
their program around traditional academic disciplines. A larger university, for example, might be
organized in colleges concerned with various social
problem themes, rather than in colleges grouped
according to disciplines.

Applying the framework, it is clear that using
a social problems approach may lead to many different combinations of curricular emphases. For
example, in terms of the locus of learning, in the
advanced stages the program will probably emphasize
experiential learning, where the student deals
directly with a pertinent social problem; before
that, however, traditional classroom learning will
probably be emphasized. In terms of the content of
the curriculum, the program, almost by definition,
includes both breadth and depth: breadth through
the delineation of a problem area within the context of a larger theme, but depth in the sense of
pursuing the problem with the aid of a limited
number of methodological approaches. Similarly,
the program is likely to be flexible, although
designated introductory courses may be required.

Possibly the best single example of a social
problems approach is the curriculum at the
University of Wisconsin--Green Bay. The focus of

the program is man and his environment. (At UWGB, "environment" is defined to include the bio-physical, social, cultural, and aesthetic spheres.) The aim of the program is to help student, instructor, and community member to relate more effectively to, and do something constructive about, the environment.

The four colleges of UWGB are organized around environmental themes rather than traditional academic disciplines. They are the College of Human Biology, the College of Environmental Sciences, the College of Community Sciences, and the College of Creative Communication. The names suggest the focus of each college and its particular area of teaching, research, and community outreach activity. A School of Professional Studies complements the theme colleges and is responsible for professional programs that relate to them.

Under the UWGB academic plan, each student builds his program around a broad problem of the physical or social environment rather than around a standard disciplinary area. He may take courses in a variety of fields, but must relate the knowledge acquired in those courses to the environmental problem chosen for the focus of study. The UWGB faculty have identified twelve broad problems, including such areas as environmental control, man's use of the natural environment, and the processes of modernization. The student chooses one of these concentration areas as his major. Within the concentration, the student may select a single subject field, such as political science, as a comajor. In addition, a concentration in almost any field may be accompanied by a professional minor that leads to a teaching certificate or credentials in business administration or other professional fields. In addition to concentration requirements, there are two major categories of All-University requirements: distribution courses and the liberal education seminar. Through the former, the University requires a student to earn a minimum of five credits in each of the four theme colleges. In some areas, concentration courses may be used to fulfill the distribution requirement.

The academic core at UWGB is the liberal education seminar (LES), a program which engages every student in a variety of learning experiences relating classic and contemporary concepts of values to contemporary environmental problems and to perennial human concerns. As a freshman, the student chooses four seven-week modules from a list of

33

topics such as the human condition in world perspective, technology and human values, resource utilization and the American character, and crises in communication.

During the intermediate years (sophomore and junior), the student learns how to become usefully involved in the community and in other cultures. Usually there is a project associated with this portion of LES, and the learner is its designer, taking major responsibility for the content and for developing skills in working with other persons outside the University. At the senior level, the student attempts to integrate his knowledge and experiences with those of students working in many other concentrations. Working with themes such as "social consciousness and the scientist," the student can apply what has been learned to continuing issues in our culture and the world. According to the catalog, "Students begin by analyzing common values and assumptions and synthesizing them into a generalized conceptual overview; return to the concrete by applying such conceptualizations to the theme; and, finally, go beyond prior assumptions by examining the nature and quality of the human condition from new perspectives." Altogether, LES is an eighteen-credit required program: freshman--six credits (two semesters); intermediate--nine credits (thematic packages, usually running two semesters plus January); senior--three credits (one semester).

In addition to UWGB, a number of other institutions have adopted a social problems thematic approach. One interesting example is the University of California at Santa Cruz. The institution is made up of eight small, self-contained, distinctive liberal arts colleges. While one of the colleges is viewed as an arts and sciences college, several of the colleges are loosely organized around a theme or social problem (e.g., science and technology, issues that confront Third World societies and the poor and powerless within this country, and development and change). Newly created colleges will address new problems. Several possible topics have been identified to serve as the basis for emerging colleges: regional planning, Pacific studies, public life, oceanographic studies, and health services.

There are some obvious advantages in using social problems as the basis for organizing the curriculum. Most important, such a problem may be a powerful force for motivating students. By

34

having a major responsibility for designing one's own program (UWGB) or by having the option of selecting a thematic program from among several major social problems (Santa Cruz), students may become more self-directed learners than they would in more traditional discipline-based programs. Coupled with experiential learning, which is usually an important component of these programs, a social problems approach is relevant to the "real world" in a way that many students desire.

Unlike most other programs, this approach tends to be heavily oriented toward the present and future. The problem orientation emphasizes a breadth of preparation that requires moving beyond the narrow sanctuaries of the academic disciplines. Such a holistic approach, which does not deny the contributions of the disciplines but rather refuses to make them the foundation of education, is appealing to those who decry the increasing fragmentation of knowledge.

At the same time, some searching questions have been raised about a social problems approach. Above all, such an approach contradicts the notion of education as a "value-free" process. Social responsibility involves a cultivation of commitment. While proponents of a social problems approach argue that value-free education is a myth, the notion persists in some circles that such an approach is inimical to a liberal arts education. In addition, critics argue that a social problems approach tends to ignore the rich historical foundations of the liberal arts in the humanities and sciences through a futuristic vision of education. Furthermore, problem-solving is only one academic skill. A curriculum that exclusively emphasizes problem-solving runs the risk of becoming excessively preoccupied with the practical. Education should be useful, but perhaps it should be much more than that. Thus, while a problems approach may be broad in its focus on issues that cut across the disciplines, it may also be excessively narrow in its emphasis on the future. Nevertheless, at the very least a social problems focus offers another major alternative approach to organizing the undergraduate program.

SELECTED COMPETENCES AS AN ORGANIZING PRINCIPLE

Some educators believe that a discipline-based approach to planning the undergraduate program is too narrow, that a "here and now" focus on developmental needs is short-sighted, that a great books approach is too past-oriented, and that a social problems focus is too value-laden. Proponents of a competence-based approach contend that the main focus of a college education should be functional; that is, the emphasis should be placed on the utility of education in later life. What should graduates be able to do? What competences should they have? And most important for our purposes, what types of curricula will assure that certain behavioral outcomes will result?

The concept of educating for competence is not new to higher education. In the 1920s, for example, the concept of a formalized competence-based curriculum for teacher education was formulated by W. W. Charters. Today, many colleges require comprehensive exams for seniors, while others utilize performance criteria in the fine arts and in technical skill areas. In recent years, however, the term "competence-based curriculum" has been given a new significance as attempts have been made to construct the entire undergraduate curriculum in terms of an explicit competence base. Bob Knott (1975) offers a useful definition of the term:

> A competence-based curriculum does not differ from other curricula in its goals. It differs in the assumption that the basic desired outcomes of an educational process can be stated in terms of defined and recognizable competences and all students can be held responsible for achieving these competences. Under a competence-based curriculum, mastery learning and not time is the major criterion of performance.

Further clarification of the concept of a competence-based curriculum can be gained by a closer examination of the joint use of the terms competence and curriculum. Competence may be defined as "the state of having requisite abilities or qualities." A curriculum is a set of designed courses or experiences. A competence-based curriculum then is one where the competences expected of all graduates are agreed upon and defined, and courses or experiences are designed to assist the student in becoming competent. If a curriculum is to have a competence base, there must be a clear statement of both what the competences are and how a student may attain them. A curriculum

designed around competences would consist of
three basic elements; first, an overall statement of competences to be acquired for a successful completion of the program; second,
sets of evaluative criteria for each competence which define the proficiency levels
required for successful attainment, and third,
sets of experiences designed to assist the
student in attaining the required competences
[p. 28].

Put simply, competence-based programs focus on
the outcomes of rather than the inputs to the
learning process. A competence-based program is
concerned with three central issues: identifying
competences, building a curriculum which will
facilitate student progress toward the achievement
of those competences, and developing adequate procedures for assessing competence.

In terms of the four curricular emphases,
competence-based programs are likely to range
across the entire length of all four of the continua. With regard to the locus of learning, most
competence-based curricula emphasize experiential
learning as much as classroom learning. Many programs, for example, give credit for previous life
experience, and most programs offer a wide variety
of experiential learning opportunities that are
compatible with identified competences. At some
colleges the program is highly individualized and
largely student-designed. In consultation with a
faculty member, the student identifies a range of
competences that he wishes to pursue, develops a
course of study designed to meet those competences,
and proposes means for assessing his progress.
Other programs, however, are faculty-designed and
allow the student considerably less freedom in
identifying individual competences to be developed.

Most competence-based programs organize their
curriculum around specific behavioral goals and
objectives. Learners are evaluated on the results
of their educational experiences in terms of the
identified competences. Demonstrable evidence, not
grades, is the sole criterion for "credit" or certification. A competence-based program can look
very much like a traditional program or can be nontraditional in a literal sense. Because the nature
of the curriculum may depend to a large extent on
whether it is faculty-designed or student-designed,
several examples will be discussed to suggest a
range of possibilities for developing a

37

competence-based curriculum.

Mars Hill College in North Carolina has recently started a competence-based curriculum wherein the college has restated its curricular requirements in terms of competences rather than simply in terms of required courses and credit hours. All bachelor degrees awarded are based on student mastery of seven basic competences. The development of the seven competence units was drawn largely from Philip Phenix's Realms of Meaning (1964) and also makes use of Arthur Chickering's Education and Identity (1969). According to the college catalog, a graduate of Mars Hill College

1....is competent in communication skills;
2....can use knowledge gained in self-assessment to further his/her own personal development;
3....comprehends the major values of his/her own and one foreign culture, can analyze relationships of values between the cultures and can appraise the influence of those values on contemporary societal developments in the cultures;
4....understands the nature of aesthetic perception and is aware of the significance of creative and aesthetic dimensions of his/her own experience which he/she can compare to other cultures;
5....understands the basic elements of the scientific method of inquiry, applies this understanding by acquiring and analyzing information which leads to scientific conclusions and appraises those conclusions;
6....has examined several attempts to achieve a unified world view and knows how such attempts are made. The graduate is aware of the broad questions that have been posed in the history, philosophy and religion of western civilization and can assess the validity of answers given to these broad questions in terms of internal consistency, comparative analyses, and his/her own position;
7....is competent in an area of specialization [Mars Hill College Emphasis, 1976, p. 6].

Proficiency in the seven areas is demonstrated by the achievement of competence units, as attested by assessment teams specializing in each of the areas, and the successful achievement of at least thirty-five course credits (or their equivalent). The assessment teams are responsible for certifying that students have demonstrated the required knowledge and skills with respect to each of the seven competences. These teams consist variously of faculty, community persons, students, and administrators according to the scope of the particular competence. They publish a list of requirements and procedures for demonstrating competence in each area. In those cases where a student successfully demonstrates competence without the use of college-designed learning experiences, the credit received is noted on the student's transcript as Credit by Examination.

In the early 1970s, Alverno College in Milwaukee, Wisconsin, fit almost perfectly the profile of a small, Catholic women's college. The majority of its students came from middle-class Catholic homes in the surrounding area. In 1973, Alverno adopted a new competence-based program that marked a radical shift in the curricular organization of the college.

To graduate from Alverno, a student must amass "competence-level units" that indicate how well she can perform tasks considered essential to a liberally educated person. Alverno has identified eight areas of competence that are required outcomes for each student who seeks a liberal education at the institution:

> Communications ability
> Analytic ability
> Problem solving ability
> Valuing in decision making
> Effective social interaction
> Understanding of the environment
> Understanding of the contemporary world
> Knowledgeable response to the arts and humanities [Alverno College Bulletin, 1976-77, p. 13].

To encourage students to structure and pace their learning as a process, each competence has six developmental levels. All students develop all eight competences through level four. In addition, they develop selected competences through level five or six, depending on their area of concentration.

At Alverno the development of competence means an individually-paced process in which the student

39

makes use of multiple resources in multiple contexts. Her courses provide a structure to assist
her in using a network of learning resources that
extend through the entire campus environment and
beyond. The student is provided with a considerable amount of practice as well as ongoing evaluation and feedback at Alverno. Texts and library
sources, media presentations, and live lectures
provide information. Laboratories, group tasks,
and off-campus sessions provide practice.
Instructors and other trained assessors provide
evaluation and feedback. Syllabi for each course
specify the possible means of learning and the
method and criteria for assessing each competence
level offered in the course.

When a student is assessed for a given competence level, she receives feedback on how she
performed in relation to the criteria specified for
that level. If her performance meets the criteria,
the specific ability is added to her record.
Students are not assigned grades to describe their
performance; verbal statements specify what they
have achieved. If the performance is not sufficient, the student receives an explanation including suggestions for learning experiences to improve
her skills before applying for reassessment.

To receive a bachelor degree from Alverno,
students demonstrate attainment of knowledge and
competence by their successful completion of forty
competence-level units. The forty units include
the first four levels of all eight competences, for
thirty-two units, plus eight advanced level units,
including at least one unit at level six. Prior to
beginning advanced level work students participate
in a seminar which enables them to evaluate their
ability in the eight general competence areas. A
major area of concentration requires the successful
completion of at least four advanced level units.
Attaining eight advanced level units enables students to complete an interdisciplinary area of concentration, or the integration of two major areas
or a major area and support areas. From this brief
description of the program, it is clear that
Alverno College provides an excellent example of
how a competence-based program might be conceived
and implemented.

In contrast to Mars Hill and Alverno,
Metropolitan State University (formerly Minnesota
Metropolitan State College) has a competence-based
program that is designed primarily by the student.
The University consciously avoided replicating

existing approaches to educating adults. In addition to being competence-based, the program has a major experiential emphasis, is student-centered, and is highly individualized.

Metropolitan State University (Metro U) has a number of fairly unique features: the absence of a traditional campus, a faculty which is drawn primarily from persons with professional backgrounds in the community, B.A. degrees awarded on the basis of demonstrated competences rather than credit hours, and a student body of which 80 percent are employed on a full-time basis. Metro U is an upper division university serving persons who wish to continue their education in times and places compatible with their lifestyles. Students enter the university after completing the first two years of college or through university recognition of learning acquired through such prior life experiences as public service, work, homemaking, or nursing education. Persons with less than two years of college or its equivalent may enroll in Metro U's model lower division competence-based programs which were developed with six area community colleges.

Metro U students must first enroll in an Individualized Educational Planning Course (IEPC) which is designed to assist students to 1) understand University policies, including assessment policies and practices; 2) learn the principles of self-directed, independent study; 3) identify their current competences and their learning needs; and 4) design their upper-division degree plans. The degree plan specifies the competences the student wants included in his upper-division program, including those gained prior to admission and those the student plans to attain while enrolled at Metro U. In addition, the degree plan specifies the learning strategies used to attain prior competences or to be used to attain future competences, the techniques that will be employed to assess the competences, and the names and qualifications of the "expert judges" who will evaluate each of the competences. Thus, the identification and articulation phases of the assessment process are accomplished through the IEPC and the development of the degree plan.

Once the IEPC is successfully completed, the student is accepted as a candidate for the Bachelor of Arts Degree, the only degree awarded by Metro U. At this point, the student assumes responsibility for and authority over his education. As a degree candidate, the student receives a faculty advisor

41

and begins to implement the degree plan using a contract learning model. Students are encouraged to use both community-based learning activities and those sponsored by the University. To facilitate the development of the University's learning resources, three Academic Conferences (Administration, Human Services, and Arts and Sciences) have been established. The Conferences coordinate the learning activities sponsored by the University and generate additional learning opportunities. Each term there is a wide variety of learning experiences offered by Metro U which may fit into a student's contract learning model, such as independent studies, internships, workshops, regular courses, and group learning opportunities. In preparation for the degree, the student must generate documentation in support of each of the competences in the degree plan. The documentation must meet the University's standards of adequate evidence and evaluators must meet the University's criteria for "expert judge." When the student has successfully demonstrated attainment of each of the competences listed in the degree plan, he is ready for graduation. In place of a credit-based letter grade transcript, Metro U uses a narrative transcript that includes the titles of the competences demonstrated, the learning strategies employed, the name and qualifications of each evaluator, and a narrative evaluation prepared by each expert judge.

Metro U offers an interesting example of an individualized competence-based curriculum. While all of the individually-designed educational programs are couched in terms of competence, they may be achieved in many ways: through prior learning, fairly traditional courses, creatively designed nonconventional experiences, or through some combination of the above. As implemented at Metro U, a competence-based curriculum is very different from the typical program of undergraduate study.

Because most of the competence-based programs are relatively new, there have been few major evaluative studies. However, proponents of such an approach have pointed out several advantages. Most significantly, they state that by clearly defining educational goals, and by stating explicitly how competences will be assessed, education can be more accountable to students and the public. By focusing on "competences" or "educational outputs," time or "credit hours" will no longer be the major evaluative mechanism for students pursuing the baccalaureate degree. The degree, in other words, will come to represent certain levels of competence rather than four years of accumulated credit hours.

Critics of such an approach are united by a nagging suspicion that one simply cannot adequately measure competence levels. After all, they say, much of learning is serendipitous and it is impossible to measure such effects. Put differently, education is a dynamic process and quantitative measurement will never capture the important qualitative learning that may be taking place. Furthermore, educational programs designed in this way run the risk of becoming just as routine and unimaginative as those where students gather credit hours. Students, being students, will learn only what they have to learn to attain certain levels of competence. They will know what they need to know, but possibly little more. As years pass and the future makes new demands, students in competence-based programs may discover that they have traded away an education for the accumulation of a handful of skills.

Nevertheless, there has been widespread acceptance of the competence-based approach and it will probably serve as one major organizing principle for the college curriculum in the foreseeable future. At the very least, such an approach has sensitized faculty and students to the importance of establishing clearly defined educational goals.

IMPLICATIONS FOR PLANNING

By comparing and contrasting the different organizing principles, relating them to the four curricular emphases, and illustrating them with concrete examples, it has been demonstrated that there can be substantial differences among the resultant curricula. There are major differences in the five organizing principles and the four curricular emphases, and the model developed here can be a useful tool for assisting academic planners in analyzing and designing various approaches to undergraduate education. The framework is an attempt to provide a lens through which the undergraduate curriculum can be brought into focus and viewed more clearly.

Confronted with these different approaches to planning the curriculum, how can faculty members and administrators utilize the model for planning their total undergraduate program? This model can be employed four distinct ways. First, it can be

43

used as a device for analyzing an institution's existing curriculum. What is the main organizing principle and what are the major curricular emphases reflected in the current curricular structure? Second, the model serves as a tool for comparing and contrasting alternative curricular arrangements--programs which reflect combinations of organizing principles and curricular emphases that are different from those currently used. Such a comparison sensitizes planners to alternative methods of organizing the curriculum.

Third, the model can be used as a heuristic device to encourage planners to think of curricular arrangements implied by combinations of organizing principles and curricular emphases which are not currently in vogue. For example, combining a great books approach with a student-designed curricular emphasis suggests a curricular structure which may not be employed currently in a college or university. Thus, using the model serves as a device for creating new curricular possibilities. Then by using the model a fourth time, planners can finally begin to construct an integrated curriculum which is based on a specified organizing principle and selected curricular emphases. Therefore, by identifying one or more organizing principles, and by consciously choosing curricular emphases and structural components which are compatible with those principles, those who plan the undergraduate curriculum will be able to develop programs which meet identified institutional needs. Surely that institution in our society which values rationality so highly must be capable of moving beyond happenstance and political gerrymandering in the development of the undergraduate curriculum.

REFERENCES

Alverno College Bulletin, 1976-77. Milwaukee, Wisconsin: Alverno College, 1976.

Chickering, Arthur W. Education and Identity. San Francisco: Jossey-Bass, 1969.

Goddard College: The Resident Undergraduate Program, 1975-1976. Plainfield, Vermont: Goddard College, 1975.

Katz, Joseph, and Nevitt Sanford. "The Curriculum in the Perspective of the Theory of Personality Development." In Nevitt Sanford (ed.), The American College. New York: John Wiley, 1962: 418-444.

King, Arthur R., and John A. Brownell. The
     Curriculum and the Disciplines of Knowledge.
     New York: John Wiley, 1966.
Knott, Bob. "What Is a Competence-Based Curriculum
     in the Liberal Arts?" Journal of Higher
     Education, 46 (1975): 25-39.
Levine, Arthur, and John Weingart. Reform of
     Undergraduate Education. San Francisco:
     Jossey-Bass, 1973.
Mars Hill College Emphasis. Mars Hill, North
     Carolina: Mars Hill College, 1976.
Pace, C. Robert. "New Concepts in Institutional
     Goals for Students." In Earl J. McGrath (ed.),
     The Liberal Arts College's Responsibility for
     the Individual Student. New York: Teachers
     College Press, Columbia University, 1966:
     38-47.
Phenix, Philip H. Realms of Meaning. New York:
     McGraw-Hill, 1964.
St. John's College Catalog, 1976-1977. Annapolis,
     Maryland: St. John's College, 1976.
The Student in Higher Education. New Haven,
     Connecticut: Hazen Foundation, 1968.

3
Liberal and General Education

What does anyone mean by "a liberal education?"
People shift their ground when they try to
explain what it is and why it is so important.
It's hard to tell whether they're talking
about subjects that can be studied in school,
such as philosophy and literature; a process
of learning or thinking; or a personal trans-
formation ("college opened my eyes"); or a
value system to which the wise and honest can
repair [Bird, 1975, p. 106].

For the better part of a decade, proponents of
liberal education have been put on the defensive.
Pressures for change in the nature and content of
curricula have resulted in the erosion or demise of
general education programs at the majority of postsecondary institutions emphasizing liberal education.

Probably the most important factor affecting
traditional conceptions of liberal education is the
changing job outlook for recent liberal arts graduates. Richard Freeman and J. Herbert Hollomon
have documented that the individual rate of return
on the college investment has dropped markedly in a
recent five-year period (from roughly 11-12 percent
in 1969 to 7-8 percent in 1974), and that "barring
unforeseen increases in demand for college graduates, their relative economic status is expected
to deteriorate moderately or remain at the present
depressed level until the end of the decade
[Freeman and Hollomon, 1975, pp. 25-28]." The
related problem of underemployment is addressed by
James O'Toole, who argues that there is "growing
evidence that this disjunction between educational
opportunity and upper-grade jobs is beginning to
create a series of potentially grave social,

46

political, and economic problems [O'Toole, 1975, p. 26]." The dual problems of unemployment and underemployment of recent graduates have undoubtedly caused many institutions to reexamine their emphasis on liberal education.

Furthermore, the erosion of the liberal arts curriculum in many institutions has paralleled the increase of "new students" in higher education: part-time, older, minority, and lower socioeconomic status learners. The new learners often desire a curriculum that is different from traditional conceptions of liberal education. Moreover, with the concomitant growth of faculty professionalization and specialization, many faculty members seem less inclined to offer general liberal arts courses or even to emphasize liberal arts preparation. Often they favor instead advanced work in a discipline or professional field.

On the other hand, the proponents of liberal education are not easily silenced, and recently a call has gone out to strengthen and revitalize general education. As an example, the council of Harvard University's faculty of arts and sciences is now considering a new proposal for a "core curriculum" to replace the general education program that has been a fixture of undergraduate life there since 1945 (Chronicle of Higher Education, March 6, 1978, p. 1). A new report on the college curriculum by The Carnegie Foundation for the Advancement of Teaching calls general education a "disaster area" and recommends that colleges provide more coherent general education programs (1977, pp. 11-18). The U.S. Commissioner of Education, Ernest L. Boyer, contends that "colleges and universities must seek to redefine the threads of common experience that bind us together [Washington Post, October 30, 1977, p. 4C]." These pronouncements, coupled with scores of articles, association meetings, and miscellaneous statements, indicate that the proponents of liberal education have shifted to the offensive.

This chapter will discuss some of the innovations that have characterized the response of many institutions to the continuing challenge of providing a program of general education. Four new approaches to general education will be identified and elaborated. As an introduction, the first section discusses the history of liberal and general education and several recent trends in general education. A final section demonstrates how the model developed in the second chapter applies to

47

planning for general education.

Before turning to a discussion of historical trends in general education, it is appropriate to raise the issue of the current meaning of the terms "liberal education" and "general education." General education goes by many names: the core curriculum, the common learning, the "required" courses. Most attempts to distinguish between general and liberal education are futile because the words have been used interchangeably by too many people for too long to lend themselves to useful distinction. For our purposes, I shall use "general education" to refer to the nonspecialized component of the degree as contrasted with the field of concentration.

A BRIEF HISTORY OF LIBERAL AND GENERAL EDUCATION

When the colonial colleges were established in America, the curriculum was directly influenced by Oxford and Cambridge and had deep roots in the medieval tradition of liberal arts. Indeed, the early curriculum was heir to the tradition of the seven liberal arts, which reaches back to the fourth and fifth centuries and the curriculum found in the Greek and Roman schools, and extends through the Middle Ages, Renaissance, and Reformation. According to Frederick Rudolph (1962):

> If Latin was the language of the Reformation, Greek and ancient Greece were the discovery of the Renaissance, and the curriculum of the colonial college necessarily made room for both. Beside the Reformation ideal of the learned clergyman was placed the Renaissance ideal of the gentleman and scholar [p. 23].

The notion that true education was liberal and general, not vocational, was reflected in the curricula of the colonial colleges. Curricular offerings were strikingly similar, usually consisting of courses in logic, religion, rhetoric, natural philosophy, mathematics, and the languages--Greek, Latin, and perhaps Hebrew (Schmidt, 1957, p. 45; Earnest, 1953, p. 22).

By the turn of the eighteenth century, the liberal arts college and the classical curriculum had been well-established in this country. But a reaction slowly grew against the narrowness and impracticality of the curriculum--a course of study

48

that lacked opportunities for specialization, failed to include applied subjects, and was often unrelated to the diverse vocational needs of students. Jacob Abbot at Amherst, George Ticknor at Harvard, and Philip Lindsley at Nashville were among the more outspoken proponents for a "parallel" course of study. Such a program was conceived not as a substitute for the classical program, but as an alternative permitting the study of modern languages, more mathematics, English, and the sciences.

Although this proposal, and other similar ones, would eventually be adopted, these reforms were forestalled by the Yale Faculty Report of 1828. In the Report, a Yale faculty committee declared that the purpose of a college education was to provide the "furniture" (factual knowledge) and "discipline" (memory, judgment, imagination, and habits of thought) of the mind. The Report argued for the prescribed curriculum, on the principle that every liberally educated person should be acquainted with certain branches of knowledge, and that the average undergraduate was not intellectually mature enough to make his own choices regarding his education. The Report did not reject advanced study in speccialized and professional fields, but argued that such studies should take place only after completion of the undergraduate liberal arts courses.

John Brubacher and Willis Rudy (1976) refer to the influence of the Report:

> This report was probably the most influential publication in the whole history of American higher education between the Revolution and the Civil War. It marked a real turning point. As a thoroughgoing defense of the traditional American liberal arts college, it gave heart to academic conservatives everywhere. To be sure, this was but a temporary stemming of the tide; nevertheless, during the ante-bellum period, the Yale pronouncement exercised great sway [p. 104].

If the Yale Report effectively stalemated major curriculum upheaval, the forces for change could not be resisted indefinitely. In the spirit of Jacksonian democracy, students and parents demanded more vocationally-oriented programs; in the same vein, many employers argued that colleges should offer more practical training to serve the nation's growing industrial needs. Responding to

these demands, many colleges gradually revised
their undergraduate program to include more emphasis on applied subjects, technical fields, and preprofessional and professional fields.

The most important single event in the gradual
unfolding of the curriculum from the general-
liberal to the utilitarian-vocational was the
Morrill Act (Land Grant Act) of 1862. The Act provided money through the sale of federal lands for
the establishment of at least one college in every
state "where the leading object shall be, without
excluding other scientific and classical studies,
and including military tactics, to teach such
branches of learning as are related to agriculture
and the mechanic arts . . . in order to promote the
liberal and practical education of the industrial
classes in the several pursuits and professions in
life [Hofstadter and Smith, 1961, p. 568]."

If the Morrill Act undercut the significance
of liberal education in favor of teaching the
"practical arts," the growing influence of German
universities--with their emphasis on specializa-
tion--also seriously threatened the preeminence of
general and liberal studies at the undergraduate
level. During the nineteenth century, roughly
9,000 Americans studied at German universities, and
a number of them were influential in grafting the
German model onto the American undergraduate curriculum.

According to Edward Blackman (1969), the
German university

> . . . assumed that the student was now, after
> graduation from the gymnasium, liberally edu-
> cated and mature enough to look after himself
> with no trace of the spirit of *in loco
> parentis*. Most important of all, the univer-
> sity was regarded as an institution where men
> learned to be highly trained specialists who
> would later do some teaching to other prospec-
> tive specialists but whose primary values were
> related to original research, the graduate
> seminar, the laboratory, the learned monograph,
> the journals, and the conventions of their dis-
> ciplines. There was no place for the kind of
> undergraduate liberal education which continued
> to form part of the undergraduate curriculum
> in the United States [p. 523].

To be sure, the German model was never whole-
heartedly adopted by the majority of American

postsecondary institutions. Nevertheless, the impact of the German university on the undergraduate curriculum was similar to the influence of the Morrill Act: specialization was strengthened at the undergraduate level and the status of the liberal arts was undermined even further.

The liberal arts were further challenged by the growth of the elective system, which was developed gradually during Charles Eliot's long tenure at Harvard University (1869-1909). By the end of Eliot's tenure as President, a Harvard student could literally take any course at all under the elective system. As a consequence, many undergraduate students chose to specialize in newly emerging fields, and this concentration was usually at the expense of general education.

These developments--the Morrill Act, the influence of the German universities, and the elective system--gradually combined to create a fear among many educators that undergraduate education would produce specialists lacking the characteristics of liberally educated persons. After the turn of the century, there was a strong reaction on the part of the advocates of "liberal culture"--those who saw liberal education being undermined by pressures for specialization and vocationalism (Veysey, 1965, pp. 180-251). Liberal education was in disarray, and many of its sympathizers joined together in the search for a response to the nagging question: Was there some way to recover the coherence of the undergraduate program through the revival of the liberal tradition? Although they could not mount a serious challenge to the alliance between utilitarianism and specialization, the proponents of liberal education were able to bring about a gradual reassertion of the importance of general education at the undergraduate level.

The first major attempt to reestablish some unity in the undergraduate program was taken in 1909 by Eliot's successor at Harvard, Abbott Lawrence Lowell. Through a faculty committee Lowell secured basic changes in Harvard's undergraduate program. To restore some notion of the common learning, a general education component of the undergraduate program, based on a distribution system, was adopted. Students in the first two years were required to choose courses in each of the major divisions of knowledge: the humanities, the social sciences, and the natural sciences. The idea of a general education program, by setting aside a segment of the student's program for general studies, marked an attempt to restore at least some measure of the common liberal arts tradition to the undergraduate program. This new pattern was adopted at most colleges and universities in the following decades. It failed, all the same, to satisfy those critics who argued that the abuses of the elective system were only partially eliminated through a system of distribution requirements which did not adequately embrace, much less define, the liberal arts tradition. According to Earl McGrath (1976):

> The distribution system . . . failed to instill the breadth of learning its advocates intended. Each student's program of studies came to have little resemblance to that of his classmates, and particularly to the required curriculum in the colleges of 1850, to say nothing of the original seven liberal arts of the early days at the University of Paris [pp. 22-23].

A more ambitious attempt to reinvigorate the liberal arts tradition led to a number of reforms, known collectively as the "general education movement," which were implemented at a variety of institutions. Beginning at Columbia College after World War I, the general education movement gradually led to the initiation of new programs at Chicago during the following decade, followed by changes at such schools as Colgate, Harvard, Michigan State, and the University of Wisconsin. All of these programs included more than a system of distribution courses. Each, in its own way, attempted to provide an integrated approach to general education. There was a shared concern for the broad outlines of knowledge, particularly the cultivation and transmission of the philosophical and intellectual inheritance of the Western world. These goals were usually achieved by developing interdisciplinary survey courses and a core curriculum in which all students participated.

A major impetus to the rapid spread of general education after World War II was a book entitled General Education in a Free Society: Report of the Harvard Committee, which appeared in 1946. By the 1950s, the movement was in its heyday and the term "general education" became more acceptable than "liberal education" largely because the latter had an elitist connotation. (For a more detailed recounting of the history of general education at

Harvard, Columbia College, and the University of Chicago, see Daniel Bell's classic study, The Reforming of General Education.)

The general education movement, as it developed in the 1940s and 1950s, proved to be relatively short-lived, however. By the early 1960s, general education programs at many institutions were being gradually dismantled. The majority of institutions followed a pattern similar to the one at Columbia: every few years an interdisciplinary course was abandoned or displaced as students were allowed to substitute discipline-based courses to satisfy their general education requirements. The notion of a common core, usually consisting of broad courses cutting across the basic academic divisions (social sciences, natural sciences, and humanities), had largely been abandoned by the end of the decade. Of course, the strengthening of academic departments may have accounted for some of these developments, for the department often seemed to work at cross-purposes to the general education movement. As Frederick Rudolph (1977) describes it in his history of the undergraduate curriculum:

> Concentration was the bread and butter of the vast majority of the professors, the style they knew and approved, the measure of departmental strength and popularity. Breadth, distribution, and general education were the hobby horses of new presidents, ambitious deans, and well-meaning humanists of the sort who were elected to curriculum committees by colleagues as a gesture of token support for the idea of liberal learning. When that gesture collided with the interests of department and the major field, only occasionally did the general prevail over the special [p. 253].

The twentieth century curricular landscape is strewn with attempts to reinvigorate the liberal learning. On the one hand, the excesses of the elective system, as it was implemented at the turn of the century, have been curbed by the establishment of what are known as "general education" programs. On the other hand, the failure of most attempts to revitalize the liberal tradition is difficult to refute. The overall fate of the general education movement, the major focus for reform in the twentieth century, is a monument to the difficulty of redefining the liberal tradition in light of our current condition.

The situation today seems not unlike that at the turn of the century, when the defenders of the liberal tradition confronted curricular disarray in the American undergraduate program. There seems to be a new sense of urgency about the condition of liberal education.

RECENT TRENDS IN GENERAL EDUCATION

Two major research studies of trends in general education were completed in the last decade. In the late 1960s, Paul Dressel and Frances DeLisle studied the undergraduate curricular requirements at 322 institutions over a ten-year period. Although they did not find any major changes in general education programs, they observed a general relaxation of specific prescriptions and requirements. The following statements summarize their major findings regarding general education requirements:

1. Formal requirements in English composition, literature, and speech have decreased.
2. Foreign language requirements have increased, with two years (or the equivalent) being by far the most common requirement.
3. The use of proficiency tests for meeting requirements in writing, speech, and foreign language has increased.
4. Requirements in philosophy and religion have been reduced with these subjects more frequently appearing as options in a distribution requirement.
5. The specification of mathematics as a requirement or an option has increased.
6. There is some tendency to reduce physical education requirements and to eliminate credits and grades for it.
7. Basic and general requirements remain at approximately 37 percent of the degree requirements and are roughly divided into 17 percent humanities and 10 percent for each of the social and natural sciences [Dressel and DeLisle, 1969, p. 30].

A more recent study, sponsored by the Carnegie Council on Policy Studies in Higher Education, examined changes in the undergraduate curriculum at 210 four-year colleges and universities between

54

1967 and 1974. Not surprisingly, the researchers found a dramatic relaxation of specific general education requirements as well as a marked decline in the proportion of undergraduate work required in general education. Most dramatically, the researchers found that the proportion of a student's undergraduate program actually devoted to general education was about 22 percent less in 1974 than in 1967, a drop of about twelve semester credit hours. Of the institutions surveyed, 72 percent showed this trend and the average decline was approximately 14 percent, with a range of 1 to 54 percent (Blackburn, Armstrong, Conrad, Didham, and McKune, 1975, p. 12).

The study also found that the general education curriculum has become much less structured. It was concluded that there has been a marked move away from specific course requirements toward distribution requirements where the student selects from a more or less specified set of course offerings. Moreover, free choice has been substantially increased in those institutions in which distribution requirements were previously the norm. In 1967, for example, the average general education requirement consisted of 50 percent prescribed courses, 46 percent distribution courses, and 4 percent free or elective courses. By 1974 the proportion of prescribed general education courses had dropped to 28 percent. There was a slight increase in distribution courses to 54 percent and a substantial increase in free courses to 18 percent (pp. 12-14).

Finally, the study looked at changes in basic requirements within general education. The researchers found that the number of institutions requiring English composition, a foreign language, and mathematics declined appreciably from 1967 to 1974: from 90 percent to 72 percent for English, from 72 to 53 percent for foreign language, and from 33 to 20 percent for mathematics. The percentage of colleges and universities requiring physical education declined from 86 to 55 percent (p. 34).

These two studies, especially the latter, suggest a considerable ferment regarding requirements in general education. Although the trend has been to decrease the number of required courses, it is difficult to predict what the future will hold. Movement away from general education is often followed by movement in the other direction. The pendulum swings, and the "currently-out-of-favor" can become the next fad. As the remainder of this

55

chapter suggests, higher education now seems to be on the threshold of a major period of innovation aimed at revitalizing the liberal arts tradition through the reform of general education.

NEW APPROACHES TO GENERAL EDUCATION

A clear indication of the spirit of reform in undergraduate education is evident in recent attempts to revise general education programs. Institutions are implementing a variety of new courses and programs that either are a relic of the past and have been revived or freshly conceived, or represent fundamentally new approaches. Senior seminars, survey courses, required courses in Western civilization or English composition, and new offerings in experience-based, values-based, or future-based courses, are among the list of innovations--though most of these have been around for generations.

Four major categories of recent innovation merit special attention: core programs, interdisciplinary programs, competence-based programs, and freshman seminars. While none of these categories is new, many of the concepts included within them represent new and different approaches to general education, especially for the majority of institutions. Viewed against the perceived erosion of general education in the sixties and seventies, these programs and courses represent concerted efforts to provide integrated and cohesive learning experiences, in a variety of ways, for students engaged in the higher learning. In the majority of cases, they represent efforts to revive the liberal tradition in a new and changing context. The following sections discuss various innovative approaches in each of the four categories.

Core Programs

In response to growing criticism of the lack of structure in their curricula, many colleges are seeking to define, once again, what should constitute the threads of common experience in an era of rapid cultural and social change and greater access to higher education. Colleges and universities across the country--from Harvard to William and Mary--have been reappraising their general education programs. Following on the heels of the relaxation of general education requirements in the

56

sixties and early seventies, the move toward core
programs represents an attempt to provide integration that has purportedly been lacking in existing
distribution and elective systems. According to
many observers, attempts to reconstruct and revive
core curricula represent the major area of innovation in undergraduate education.

A "core" curriculum is a common set of related
experiences, designed to achieve specific purposes.
In that all students must participate in them,
these integrated experiences are prescribed. Within
the prescribed framework, however, core curricula
can also include some options for student choice,
such as distribution offerings in circumscribed
areas.

The current U.S. Commissioner of Education,
Ernest L. Boyer, is among the most visible proponents of the movement toward reestablishing core
programs. In a provocative piece entitled
Educating for Survival, Boyer and Martin Kaplan suggest that "our own social and cultural condition
calls out for a new core curriculum [Boyer and
Kaplan, 1977, p. 56]." While they propose a new
core program, the authors' main contribution is to
raise the central issue confronting those attempting to develop core curricula: What are the common
experiences, in light of our own social and cultural
condition, that could become the new center of general and liberal education? Clearly the success of
current attempts to provide common experiences
relies to a great extent on the ability of curriculum reformers to identify and implement new bases
for integration.

Institutions employ two major approaches in
organizing core programs. One approach attempts to
define a common curriculum that does not perpetuate
the established disciplinary hierarchies that have
made general education programs vulnerable in the
past. This approach involves designing an interdisciplinary core, built upon one or more themes
which cut across traditional academic departments
and common divisional arrangements.

The second approach to redesigning the core is
more eclectic, often including but not limited to
interdisciplinary components. Such an approach
frequently incorporates a combination of special
subjects (such as English composition), survey
courses (such as Western civilization), discipline-
based courses, and interdisciplinary courses (such
as freshman or senior seminars). While the components of the core may vary considerably from one

institution to another, these programs are usually integrated around a set of principles or axioms about what constitutes an educated person in the last quarter of the twentieth century. It is instructive to review several illustrations of these approaches, beginning with two examples of an interdisciplinary common core.

Warner Pacific College is a coeducational church-related liberal arts college located in Portland, Oregon. As the result of a major curriculum review, the College has implemented an interdisciplinary core curriculum entitled the Culture of Western Man (CWM). Since the inception of the program four years ago, CWM has been a catalyst for major changes in the entire academic program, including the development of six academic centers in place of traditional divisions and departments.

The Culture of Western Man program rests on the philosophic foundation that man's knowledge is a whole which cannot be categorized into separate and often disparate "disciplines" without great loss to both the student and the material under consideration. The process of integration is achieved through a problem-oriented structure which encourages holistic thinking. By arranging the program according to related topics rather than chronological progression, significant problems of the human experience are addressed from a variety of perspectives. Examples include: Is man morally bound? Do the arts affect values? Do faith, sense, perception and reason always lead to the same conclusion? Are there alternatives to the modern industrial state? What is obscenity?

The Culture of Western Man program is organized around twelve general topics including: the Nature of Civilization, the Nature of Western Lifestyles, the Nature of Political Power and Political Theory, the Nature of Social Organization, the Nature of Religion, the Nature of Man's Artistic Expression, the Nature of Nature, the Nature of Life, the Nature of Man's Environment, the Nature of Economic Man, the Nature of Human Conflict, and the Nature of Man's Questions about Himself. Each of these general areas is divided into ten specific topics, with the six-quarter core program integrating the study of history, political science, philosophy, religion, psychology, literature, sociology, economics, and science.

The format of the Culture of Western Man program is designed not only to break down disciplinary barriers but also to provide varied learning

experiences. In a section of the program devoted
to the study of Western lifestyles, for example,
students spend one week on the specific topic: How
has Western man come to see the material and spiritual worlds as rivals? Students begin the week by
listening to lecturers from science and religion
deal with specific aspects of the question. For
example, the representative from religion lectures
on the Christian view of the physical world. All
participating faculty attend this opening forum on
Monday of each week. In addition to the lecture
format, the forum may include a variety of
approaches such as roundtable or panel discussions
and media presentations. Regardless of the method
of presentation, the main purpose of the forum is
to introduce the question area for the week by presenting significant authorities in the particular
area of investigation.

The greater part of the student's time is
spent in independent study. Each week the student
is introduced to selections from recognized authors
who have contributed to man's understanding of the
issue under examination. Participants also take
advantage of contemporary media resources chosen
from available cassettes, slide and filmstrip series,
and films. A guide for the study of readings and
media presentations is prepared by the faculty and
included in the student handbook. Each week students respond in a personal journal to the readings
and media resources. This exercise is a means of
expressing one's reactions and it also helps the
faculty to trace student development. In addition,
there is an independent research option which
enables students to contract and complete a
research paper or media-oriented project.

Participation in a discussion group is the
climax of each week. Students discuss their observations and conclusions in a small group consisting
of their peers and a faculty member. While the
faculty member helps to define the issues and facilitate group processes, the main purpose of the
session is to provide the opportunity for student-
initiated discussion related to the week's question.
These meetings, reflecting the goals of the CWM program, emphasize "values" through student participation in such exercises as simulation-gaming and
"values-clarification."

To summarize, the Culture of Western Man program
at Warner Pacific is an interesting example of an
interdisciplinary core curriculum. By requiring
all students to participate in a common program

which is integrated by topics rather than academic disciplines, CWM illustrates how one institution has attempted to forge a new way of integrating liberal and general education for all its students.

Saint Joseph's College, located in Rensselaer, Indiana, adopted a Core Program because it was seen to be a better way of achieving the goals of the institution than distributive approaches to general education.* The Core Program is integrative, giving the entire student body and participating faculty a common experience in reflecting on man, his situation, his civilization and culture, his achievements and problems, his meaning and purpose.

In order to offset the trend toward specialization or vocational training in most of American higher education, the Core is strongly generalist and humanistic. It emphasizes the goal of becoming a "self worth being," of leading a genuinely human existence, as the basic issue of liberal education. Although the content of each semester of Core varies, the program maintains an overall common and constant concern for human values.

The Core Progarm replaces what used to be a 54-credit, predominantly lower-level and distributive approach to general education with a 45-credit, integrative, and interdisciplinary set of semester programs distributed evenly over the four years of college education. In place of a required number of courses from several separate departments, Core involves a 6-credit interdisciplinary course in all but the last of the eight semesters taken by the student. The structure of the Core Program is displayed below:

Freshmen: Core 1--The Contemporary Situation
                 (6 credits)
               Core 2--Hebrew and Graeco-Roman
                 Heritage (6 credits)
Sophomores: Core 3--The Middle Ages (6 credits)
               Core 4--The Modern World (6
                 credits)
Juniors: Cores 5 & 6--Man in the Universe
                 (6 credits)

---

*The following description of the program has been adapted from a speech given by Dr. John P. Nichols, Professor of Philosophy and Core Curriculum Coordinator, at a recent meeting of the Association for General and Liberal Studies.

                    Cores 7 & 8--Non-Western Studies
                    (6 credits)
      Seniors: Core 9--Toward a Christian
                    Humanism (6 credits)
                    Core 10--Christianity and the
                    Human Situation (3 credits)

     As a complement to this brief listing of the
individual segments of Core, it is important to
stress the overall integration of the segments into
a single general education program which has a def-
inite rationale and developmental unity operating
throughout all four years. The following para-
graphs should clarify the overall thrust of the
Core Program.
     The first semester of the freshman year begins
with "The Contemporary Situation" because the main
objective given to Core 1 is self-discovery and
self-assessment. The student is invited to take
inventory of his personal and communal problems and
resources: As a young man or woman in twentieth
century America, what outlooks and values have I
adopted? What can we reasonably expect to achieve
in the remaining years of this century? What are
the prospects and hopes for creating a meaningful
personal existence and a just society?
     The time span covered by Core 1 extends back
to 1900, not for arithmetic convenience or to
relieve other Cores of some years of content, but
to attain a very specific purpose. The student's
edifice of meaning was constructed under the influence of his parents and grandparents, as well as
that of peers, teachers, and so on. By becoming
acquainted with the events and hopes and crises of
those immediately ancestral generations, the student can begin to discover the impact of the past
on his living present, the relevance of history to
human existence. This is not approached in service
to any particular philosophy of history but in
terms of the simple fact of life that our meanings
are shared meanings and that our existence is an
historical existence. The complement to the
forward-looking dimension of hope in human existence is the retrospective dimension of memory.
With the establishment of this dialectic between
hope and memory, Core 1 opens the student up to the
historical sections of Core in the following three
semesters.
     Cores 2, 3 and 4--the second semester of the
freshman year and the two semesters of the

                         61

sophomore year--seek to encounter the origins of Western civilization and follow its subsequent development. At the end of Core 4 the student has worked his way, hopefully with enriched historical understanding and development of critical acumen, back to the starting point of Core 1.

Although Cores 1 through 4 attempted to deal with 4,000 years of Judeo-Christian tradition and 2,800 years of Western Culture, a still greater challenge to the student's imagination and sensitivity awaits him in the junior year. Non-Western Core (Cores 7 & 8) transports the student out of the West, inviting him to meet and learn to appreciate fellow human beings who have created cultures quite different from his own. The great cultures of India, China, Africa and Japan, whether in terms of complements, contrarieties, or correctives, have much to teach us, in spite of our boasts of Western superiority.

In addition, the "Story of Man" that science tells, in the concurrent Core Science segment (Cores 5 & 6), is a story of billions of years of cosmic and biological evolution. It speaks of a cosmos of fantastic dimensions but which is still man's home. If Cores 2, 3 and 4 put us in touch with our cultural roots, Core Science reveals how intimately our human lives are connected with all of life and with basic cosmic processes--our cosmic and biological roots. The two programs of the junior year do, however, converge--whether by political, economic, ecological, metaphysical, or religious paths--on the reality of the oneness of the family of man.

Finally, the first three years of Core (Cores 1 through 8) can be regarded as more analytic than anything else, in the sense that these cores provide information about, perspective on, and appreciation of all things human. The senior year proposes to tie together all of the preceding materials of the Core Program in a synthesis that is deeply and thoroughly Christian. Core 9 works at such a synthesis in terms of theory and principle, whereas Core 10 applies those principles in a spirit of Christian responsibility in a world where man is assuming conscious and deliberate control of the course of evolution.

Another rather interesting perspective on the total Core Program lies in the broadening and deepening of awareness that occurs as the students move from one semester to the next. The focus of the content of the Core segments and the invitation to value commitment grow significantly from semester to semester. In Core 1, the focus is the "self" in twentieth century America; Cores 2 through 4 broaden that perspective to include the origins, development and recent condition of "The West"; in the junior year the student is invited to cope with the concepts of "cosmos" and "Spaceship Earth"; and in Cores 9 and 10 questions of ultimate meaning and deepest commitment are treated, the "Alpha and Omega" of human existence and "the one thing necessary" of the New Testament.

The mechanics of the Core Program are structured in such a way as to respect both the interdisciplinary and the humanist dimensions of Core. The typical 6-credit segment of Core involves four contact hours per week: two hour-long lectures in the College Auditorium (at which the entire freshman, sophomore, junior, or senior class is in attendance), and two hour-long discussions in a group of about eighteen students and one professor. What might at first seem to be an overly generous allocation of credit hours to the normal semester of Core--six credits for four contact hours--is justified in view of the large amount of reading and writing assigned in the program. And though the preceding comment seems to emphasize individual student work, it is generally in the discussion sessions that the readings, the lectures, and the student's own reflections really come into focus.

The roles of a faculty member in the two scheduled parts of Core are quite different. As a lecturer in the auditorium meetings, the professor presents himself as an expert in commenting on a reading assignment or a related topic in a scholarly yet pedagogically appropriate fashion. In the discussion situation, however, the professor often has to assume the position of a colearner, since the topic under discussion may well come out of a field of study which is not his own area of specialization. The different types of faculty-to-faculty and student-to-faculty relationships which this structure demands and favors have revitalized the academic community of Saint Joseph's College.

Saint Joseph's College is committed to the Core curriculum and the humanizing and liberating educational experience which it represents. The Core expresses this college's manner of structuring a liberal arts education which respects both the concern for human values of the liberal arts tradition and the need to give new life to liberal education in the last quarter of the twentieth century.

Emory and Henry College, located in Emory, Virginia, has recently completed a major curriculum review. A new curriculum, including a core segment, was introduced in the fall of 1978 and will be fully implemented by the fall of 1980.

The new Emory and Henry curriculum is being constructed around five goals or "pillars" of education. The first pillar involves the pragmatic goal of education--career development, the reasonable match between educational preparation and work opportunities. The second pillar, closely related to the first, is the concept of service. A job or career must produce something more than self-gratification. The highest joy comes from work which satisfies self yet also serves other persons. The third pillar is concerned with intellectual excellence and academic integrity; it involves the central goal of education--teaching students how to think and learn. The fourth pillar focuses on the spiritual and ethical side of life, recognizing that liberal arts colleges must take the lead in strengthening society's ethical framework. Emory and Henry is committed to the study of value and ethical principles, encouraging students to consider the implications of their actions and beliefs. The fifth pillar relates to developing mental resilience and a love of lifelong learning. The College expects each student to become acquainted with primary areas of inquiry, yet there is also the realization that the college years can provide only a modest introduction to the excitement of a limitless intellectual quest.

These pillars represent five principles which guided Emory and Henry in the consideration of curricular change. The resulting academic program has several interesting features. One of the distinguishing characteristics is that education is viewed as a joint venture for students and faculty rather than a task left solely to the professors. The curriculum is oriented toward the development of the personality structures of both students and faculty, and it is organized with specific attention to both how students learn and how knowledge is organized. A variety of educational experiences and processes is provided, designed to form a coherent unit, an integrated liberal education.

Another important characteristic of the new educational program is its focus. Each area of the curriculum is appreciated for its individual significance but also for its interrelatedness with other parts of the program. The curriculum is viewed in terms of relationships and not merely as individual courses haphazardly offered and organized. One result of this well-defined focus is the movement away from the old half-and-half concept of the four-year degree program, in which the first two years centered on education in the liberal arts and the last two years were given to the area of specialization. The Emory and Henry curriculum discards this pattern and correlates curricular structure with the developmental needs of the students. The liberal and general studies program under the new curriculum is spread over four years, as are the courses taken in the concentration area. Both in general studies and in the specialized concentration area courses are designed to respond to varying stages of student development.

For example, freshmen can be said to be in a "romantic" stage, characterized by a quest for discovery, a search for answers, and creative impulses. Emory and Henry's program responds to this sense of quest by offering freshman studies courses which in many instances have a cross-disciplinary approach to important subjects and problems. Sophomores and juniors typically may be in a second stage which emphasizes a desire for precision and specialization along with the ability to deal with complexities and a high degree of differentation. Emory and Henry encourages students at this point to pursue more in-depth courses in their concentration area, focusing on preprofessional training and skills. Also, such students are offered general studies in topics such as the great books, religion, and value inquiry. Senior students often enter a third stage, one of generalization in which each student seeks to make use of his newly acquired knowledge, capabilities, and competences. To promote such generalization and application of skills, Emory and Henry's general studies program is providing for special senior divisional seminars and global studies.

All three stages seek a synthesis between two basic functions of knowledge: the practical and the imaginative. The practical function of knowledge permits the student to use that knowledge to master his environment and his inner world. Through the imaginative function of knowledge, the individual student achieves the means to extend his real world and, in a sense, to make new worlds. This is done by the enrichment of reality and by lifting oneself beyond the immediate experiences of life.

While recognizing that the new curriculum at

Emory and Henry encompasses the total undergraduate experience, the general studies program is our primary area of interest. The purpose of the general studies courses is to provide: 1) a meaningful intellectual encounter with major fields of knowledge; 2) an interchange between knowledge and values, and the application of classroom studies to individual and societal concerns; 3) a climate which encourages the development of a personal world view and ethical consciousness; 4) a knowledge of the representative creative and intellectual developments of major cultural traditions; 5) a sense of historical perspective; 6) competence in written communication; and 7) an introduction to major areas of concentration and to professional and career goals.

The following courses, representing a total of twelve out of the thirty-eight courses required for graduation, are included in the general studies program:

> Writing Program: one course, taken during the freshman year.
> Freshman Studies: three courses, one from each division, taken during the freshman year.
> Disciplinary Studies: three courses, one from each division, normally taken during the freshman year.
> (Freshman Studies and Disciplinary Studies must be selected from the offerings of six different departments.)
> Great Books: one course, normally taken during the sophomore year.
> Religion: one course, normally taken during the sophomore year.
> Value Inquiry Studies: one course, normally taken during the junior year.
> Global Studies: one course, normally taken during the senior year.
> Divisional Seminar: one course, normally taken during the senior year.

Of the twelve, three specific courses are required for all students: the writing program, the great books course, and the religion course. Students are given several options in satisfying the remaining course requirements.

The general studies program at Emory and Henry presents a sharp contrast to the general education programs at Warner Pacific and Saint Joseph's College. Instead of relying exclusively on

66

interdisciplinary studies, the Emory and Henry program includes a variety of courses: special subjects (writing program), discipline-based subjects (disciplinary studies), and interdisciplinary subjects (global studies). Moreover, it is not a core curriculum in the strictest sense, for it allows for some student choice within certain areas while avoiding the overtones of a distribution system. Nevertheless, it is unified by a set of integrating principles which give shape and meaning to a common set of experiences. Because it is purposely eclectic in content organization and allows for some student choice, the Emory and Henry program is probably more typical of many of the emerging core curricula than the wholly prescribed, interdisciplinary-based programs at Warner Pacific College and Saint Joseph's College.

At this juncture, it is difficult to make judgments about the effectiveness of recent efforts to institute core programs. Many of these programs are still in their infancy, and most institutions are still as involved in justifying as in evaluating their efforts to invigorate the liberal tradition. Still, it is helpful to look at these reforms in light of earlier attempts at reforming general education.

Surely the most pervasive criticism of core programs comes from proponents of the "individualization" of learning; the notion of a common core is anathema to this group of reformers. Perhaps the most telling criticism of the new core program is that they do not always represent new ways of integrating general education. All too frequently some of the new programs, especially those which employ an eclectic approach to integration, seem only to clothe the same old curriculum in more prescriptive requirements and flowery prose serving mainly to disguise the absence of a new integrating principle. While an "innovative" program may seem appealing to both faculty and students, if it fails to plan on the basis of new integrating principles it may also fail to profit by the lessons of previous attempts to offer common curricula. In the twentieth century, for example, the most conspicuous attempt at integration, the "general education movement," failed at least partly because its proponents were not able to provide viable integrating principles. A good example is the Harvard general education model of the 1940s with its emphasis on Western civilization, which proved to be relatively short-lived even though it captured the imagination of numerous curriculum reformers and was implemented at many institutions.

There is a second lesson that may be gleaned from earlier attempts to build a common core. Joseph Ben-David, commenting upon twentieth century efforts to provide a common core of experiences, notes that many proponents "claimed for themselves the monopolistic authority of experts in matters that were very often beyond the pale of any expertise [Ben-David, 1972, p. 65]." Today, many reformers are perhaps given too much to exorbitant claims which may serve only to heighten expectations concerning current efforts at reform that are unrealistic given the recent history of failure to provide common learning experiences.

Still, many proponents of a core curriculum are less strident in their claims, and there is reason to believe that the current interest in core curricula will result in well-designed attempts to offer new core programs without the need for extravagant claims. More fundamentally, there is evidence to suggest that many of the new core curricula are being newly designed in light of "our own social and cultural condition." The examples discussed in this section--Warner Pacific, Saint Joseph's, and Emory and Henry--suggest that successful core curricula can be designed on new bases. However, such programs, no matter how imaginatively and thoughtfully designed, must face the litmus test of their effectiveness in practice. Whether or not these and other core programs continue to survive and be effective, or whether they will suffer the fate of most twentieth century attempts to provide a common core, remains to be seen. There is reason for optimism, but optimism tempered by the lessons of the recent past.

Putting these caveats aside, there seems to be a number of advantages to developing a core program. Most important, a unified curricular concept may increase the likelihood that students will have a unified undergraduate experience that is explicitly based upon shared conceptions of the purposes of general education. As a consequence, the curricular program and mission of the college will be easier to interpret to prospective students. In addition, the establishment of core curricula to serve preferred goals will help institutions to develop clear criteria by which to evaluate programs and student performance. In a time characterized by strident calls for academic "accountability," core curricula can provide institutions with both the substance and method of response.

Interdisciplinary Programs

In addition to interdisciplinary core curricula, there are a variety of other new interdisciplinary approaches to general education. Proponents of these approaches, while rejecting the idea of a common core required of all students, are nonetheless committed to program integration through the use of interdisciplinary approaches. They often argue that greater educational benefits are derived from courses and programs which treat knowledge from related fields simultaneously rather than in disciplinary isolation. Although academic disciplines provide important constructs for doing research and disseminating new knowledge, the important issues in life, including most current problems, do not present themselves in neat disciplinary packages. The truly important issues facing mankind require a broad, interdisciplinary perspective.

The main characteristic of interdisciplinary programs is that the focus for instruction is drawn from a variety of subject disciplines rather than a single one. These programs are organized around a theme or problem, or sometimes a cluster of themes or problems, that cut across traditional academic disciplines. Some of the perennially popular themes, such as historical periods or civilizations, reflect traditional approaches to integration. Increasingly, however, institutions have sought to carve out new themes (such as the role of values in modern society) or problems (such as man and his environment) as vehicles of integration.

Interdisciplinary core programs, which were discussed in the previous section, are among the most popular of the new interdisciplinary approaches. But three alternative interdisciplinary patterns, in which students have some choice, have emerged in the past several years. These programs are similar in that they offer students an alternative, or set of alternatives, to required core curricula or other patterns of general education requirements. First, an increasingly common interdisciplinary program is one in which students satisfy their general education requirements through studying a particular theme or problem in lieu of prescribed courses, distribution requirements, etc. An example of this approach, the "Concourse" program at the Massachusetts Institute

69

of Technology, is discussed below.

Second, many programs offer students several themes or problems from which to satisfy their general education requirements, although additional requirements must occasionally be met. The "Integrated Studies" program at the University of Denver, also discussed below, is an example of this approach.

Third, there are a number of programs in which students design their own interdisciplinary program around a theme or problem. In most cases, this student-designed program is offered as an option alongside extant general education requirements. In the majority of cases, a program of general studies is agreed upon through an individualized learning contract between the student and a faculty member or a committee of faculty. These student-designed programs are being used at several of the more innovative institutions in the country: Empire State College, the New College at the University of Alabama, and the University-without-Walls (Union for Experimenting Colleges and Universities). In most cases, a student-designed general education program is part of an individualized or student-designed degree program. (For examples of student-designed degree programs, which usually encompass student-designed general education components, the reader should consult chapter six.)

Concourse is an alternative to the regular freshman general education program at the Massachusetts Institute of Technology (MIT). The Concourse Program gives the same credits and offers the same material, problems, and examinations as the standard freshman curriculum. The differences lie in the approach and the teaching method. The courses are organized so as to interact with each other to reflect some central theme, which for the past several years has been "Mind, Machine, and Meaning." In order to study the workings of computers and the physiology of the brain, and to understand where principles are similar and where they are different, one needs all the sciences. One also needs philosophy, the history of ideas, world literature, a feeling for language, and, in short, all the amenities of a humanistic education.

Concourse currently operates under the administrative aegis of the Department of Electrical Engineering and Computer Science, though participating faculty are drawn from throughout the University. This program is not designed for large classes, so registration has been limited to approximately fifty students. Over 350 students applied to participate during the 1977-1978 academic year, with the final participants eventually selected by lottery.

In addition to a Science Core, Concourse is composed of a Humanities Core and a Concourse Elective. During the 1977-1978 academic year, the Humanities Core was based on an experimental curriculum being developed in MIT's Technology Studies Program. This is an American Civilization curriculum, with sharp focus on the technological underpinnings of modern life. The general theme was "Mechanization, Industrialization, Automation," and the central concern was the effects of these processes on culture as a whole--its social, economic, aesthetic, ethical, as well as technical origins and ramifications. Some subthemes included were: the interrelations between organic and mechanic systems, American utopias, romanticism and realism in literature and life, the nature of work and history.

The readings were drawn from a wide variety of literary and historical sources, as well as from the works of contemporary observers. For example, students began with Kurt Vonnegut's Player Piano and Joseph Weizenbaum's Computer Power and Human Reason. Then the course jumped backward to the early nineteenth century to look at the process of industrialization from the point of view of the first Americans who experienced it. Students read diaries of farmers and mill workers, took a field trip to the agrarian museum at Old Sturbridge Village, and visited a working textile mill in Lowell, the first industrial city in the New World. The first semester dealt with the development of the textile and steel industries, the second semester with the automobile and computer industries.

The Concourse Elective is a set of regularly scheduled sessions which involve Concourse students and a sizable group of faculty. Students explore intensively a number of selected topics that have both broad educational value and specific relevance to the scientific and technical fields which most students enter during their MIT education. As noted earlier, a recent theme was "Mind, Machine, and Meaning." Subtopics within the general theme included: computation, perception, the mind-body problem, information theory, physiological psychology, the structure of history, and the uses and construction of models.

71

The meetings in the Concourse Elective consist of lectures, discussions, seminars, debates, and dramatizations, in varying format--whatever is appropriate to the subject matter for a given day. In addition, the program takes advantage of the intellectual resources in the academic community by inviting guest lecturers to speak about their current work. Class size varies with the daily format from a maximum of fifty students in open lectures, to fifteen students in seminar and problem solving sessions, to one-on-one tutorials.

There is an important informal aspect of the Concourse Program which the faculty emphasize and encourage. These are special activities in which students may participate as individuals or in groups. For example, research opportunities exist with the Concourse faculty and any other MIT faculty member under a special program. These projects may be suggested by the faculty supervisor or they may be directly related to a student's particular interests. Concourse also runs workshops in such areas as computer programming, photography, writing, drama, and other activities centered on areas of mutual student-faculty interest.

Another new interdisciplinary program is the "Integrated Studies" program at the University of Denver. Integrated Studies are a special series of courses offered by the College of Arts and Sciences in the Humanities, the Sciences, and the Social Sciences. These block courses are offered as an optional alternative to the regular general education requirements. Each course totally satisfies the college's general educational requirement in one of these three areas and is worth fifteen quarter hours for one academic quarter, with three separate grades given for each of the five-hour parts of a given course. The subject is studied from the perspectives of teachers from various disciplines. This multidisciplinary approach attempts to provide an integration of methods, points of view and materials not commonly found in traditional three-, four-, or five-hour courses.

During the 1977-1978 academic year, students participating in the Integrated Studies program were given several course options. For example, Humanities offerings included: Classical Athens, Mexico in the Twentieth Century, Victorian America, Elizabethan England, Sung China, and the French Enlightenment. Science offerings included: The Age of Newton, Energy, and Scientific Foundations of Industrial Society. Social Sciences courses

72

included Limits to Growth and the Politics of Scarcity: Toward the Year 2000. To illustrate the interdisciplinary character of these offerings, an example of a course in each of the three areas is discussed. These examples, drawn from courses offered during the past academic year, illustrate the interdisciplinary thrust of the program.

"Energy," a science block course, is an attractive option for many students in the Integrated Studies program. Energy lends itself naturally to integrated study in the sciences. From its fundamental definitions, the concepts of potential and kinetic energy, the governing laws of thermodynamics pertaining to heat, work, and entropy of the universe, to the chemistry of combustion and the conversion of energy from one form to another; to nuclear reactors and the controversy associated with their safety; and finally to the dimunition of fossil fuels and energy bearing minerals, the concept of energy calls forth the talents of the geologist, the geographer, the chemist, the mathematician, the physicist, and the biologist. In this block, the science of energy is approached from these various points of view; energy alternatives are explored and students experiment with solar and wind energy conversion.

A recent Social Sciences Block course was "Limits to Growth and the Politics of Scarcity: Toward the Year 2000." World population and human demands are growing exponentially; earth's ecological system is threatened and natural resources are diminishing. The evolving worldwide sociopolitical order has reached the stage in which the old concepts of progress and material growth seem no longer pursuable. What is the extent of the current crisis? Will the world eventually split apart in conflict over the distribution of its shrinking resources? Has modern civilization begun to outlive its usefulness, and if so, what are the alternatives? These questions are dealt with through the studies and theories of anthropologists, sociologists, and political economists in this interdisciplinary course.

Especially because the Integrated Studies program grew out of a humanities program (and retains a major emphasis on the humanities), mention should be made of one Humanities Block course. The "French Enlightenment" examines French civilization after 1750; the concepts of "liberty, equality, brotherhood," derived from the social and political thought of the French Enlightenment, are explored

73

in depth. The full range of eighteenth century French civilization is considered: government, literature, the theatre, the visual arts, and music.

After suggesting several ways of organizing interdisciplinary programs, it is useful to discuss briefly the advantages and disadvantages of these programs. A major advantage is that such programs can address themes or problems which are only incompletely addressed by traditional academic disciplines. In the process, they offer the possibility of cultivating an appreciation of the interrelatedness of knowledge that is difficult, if not impossible, to convey in discipline-based programs. Participating faculty may also reap substantial benefits as they seek to redefine their own disciplines in light of their interdisciplinary involvement, encouraging introspection at the departmental level which may, in turn, lead to innovative approaches to departmental courses.

Interdisciplinary programs can also be a potential tool for bringing together various academic constituencies. Professors from the social sciences, natural sciences, and humanities may investigate topics which encourage a multiplicity of perspectives, serving to break down the alleged barriers between the sciences and the humanities through an ongoing dialectic. Interdisciplinary programs also offer a built-in mechanism for curricular reform, for new topics can be more easily assimilated into this structure than in discipline-based programs.

In addition, interdisciplinary programs can serve as a major source of motivation for students, because they focus on issues and problems rather than on a carefully circumscribed body of knowledge as in a discipline-based approach. Finally, interdisciplinary approaches are often accompanied by innovative approaches to instruction.

What is most appealing about many of the new interdisciplinary programs is that they represent fundamentally new approaches to integration. By way of contrast, the general education movement of the earlier part of the twentieth century was largely made up of interdisciplinary programs that were based in the divisions: natural sciences, social sciences, and humanities. In the late 1930s, for example, the widely-regarded program in general education at Columbia College required students to take broad interdisciplinary courses in each of the three major divisions. Although some institutions today offer interdisciplinary courses that do not extend beyond the boundaries of these academic divisons, there is a trend away from the survey approach to knowledge toward more clearly defined themes or problems. Thus, many of the new inter- disciplinary approaches cut across academic divi- sions, an approach that was only infrequently used in earlier general education programs. The diver- sity of interdisciplinary approaches, based on a variety of themes or problems, at least offers the possibility that many of these programs may eventu- ally prove more successful than earlier attempts at integration.

A number of criticisms have been articulated against interdisciplinary approaches. Perhaps the most outspoken critics are the staunch defenders of traditional academic departments, who view these programs as a threat to departmental hegemony. Their most strident argument is that the communica- tion of knowledge should employ the same vehicle-- the academic department--that promotes the acquisi- tion of knowledge. Of course, many of these critics fail to realize, or at least acknowledge, the potential benefits to departments as a result of participation in interdisciplinary programs.

Still, there are a number of practical prob- lems with interdisciplinary programs. Most impor- tant, these efforts are rarely effective unless participating faculty receive strong institutional support. In most institutions, the departmental structure is the major mechanism for rewarding faculty; unless faculty participating in time- consuming interdisciplinary programs receive ade- quate support, they will generally be less than enthusiastic in their involvement. In many instances, it is difficult to recruit faculty in the first place without ensuring a substantial mea- sure of reward for participation.

There are two other problems worth mentioning. First, it is often difficult to find appropriate reading for interdisciplinary courses, though this may be changing as potentially useful books (such as Jacob Bronowski's The Ascent of Man) make their way into the accepted literature. Second, estab- lishing a common language among faculty from dif- ferent disciplines presents formidable problems; conceptual and methodological differences between social scientists may be as marked as those between physicists and historians. Nevertheless, many advocates are convinced that potential problem areas can be successfully anticipated and resolved, allowing institutions to forge interdisciplinary

programs which offer meaningful alternatives to
distribution programs of general education.

Competence-Based Programs

As competence-based programs have gradually
gained a foothold throughout academe, some have
been initiated in a number of colleges as the basis
of the general education program. A major impetus
for the movement toward competence-based general
education has come from the Fund for the Improvement
of Postsecondary Education (FIPSE), a federal
agency designed to support educational innovations.
In 1974, the Fund provided eighteen grants totaling
$1.6 million for projects that involved competence-
based education, and funding has continued in the
last several years. Harold Hodgkinson reported
that by 1975 more than 200 institutions were using
or seriously considering adopting some form of
competence-based education.

The movement toward competence-based education
often brings together a group of "old" reformers
who seek alternatives to the academic disciplines
as the basis for liberal learning and a group of
"new" reformers who think that colleges should be
more accountable for the claims they make to students and the public. Because they define general
education in terms of outcomes or competences--
such as effective communication skills, analytic
ability, or problem-solving skills--these programs
are called competence-based.

In general, competence-based programs are
based on institutionally-derived competence levels
which students must meet in order to complete their
general education requirements. Although institutions offer a wide variety of methods to validate
student competence, the various programs are united
by a commitment to assess and evaluate student competences in terms of specific tasks or skills
designed by the college.

In its recent report on the college curriculum,
The Carnegie Foundation for the Advancement of
Teaching (1977) identifies several important ways
in which competence-based curricula are different
from traditional subject-based curricula:

1. They are directed toward the achievement
    of outcomes that are explicitly defined
    and made known to students in advance.
2. They recognize competences wherever they
    are achieved--in class, in class at

another institution, through work experience, or through some other learning activity.
3. There is (theoretically) no time schedule for the completion of the program.
4. They are sometimes developed in ways that assess the margin of competence specifically added by the college experience and are thus adapted to each individual. In such cases, a diagnostic assessment is made when the student begins the program, and a summational assessment is made when he or she completes it.
5. They endeavor to assess not only the student's cognitive development, as evidenced by what they know, but also their affective development, as evidenced by the manner in which they perform [pp. 125-126].

Aside from the focus on competences and evaluation, these programs are as diverse as more traditional types of general education. For example, some programs place considerable emphasis on experiential learning, while others emphasize traditional classroom learning. Also, there is considerable variation in the competences identified across institutions. The major differences between many of the programs lie in the variety of nontraditional methods used to assess student competence. Some programs utilize comprehensive examinations, others use groups of faculty assessors, and still others rely on traditional term papers and grades. Despite their surface similarity to traditional general education plans, competence-based programs differ markedly in their emphases on competences and evaluation.

In addition to the competence-based degree programs discussed in the second chapter (Alverno College, Mars Hill College, and Metropolitan State University), a number of other colleges have adopted competence-based general education programs: Oklahoma City University, Brigham Young University, Sterling College, and Our Lady of the Lake University.

In 1975 the faculty of Our Lady of the Lake University in San Antonio approved a resolution establishing a competence-based general education program. The resolution was the culmination of a year-long planning effort made possible by a grant from the Fund for the Improvement of Postsecondary

Education.

Our Lady of the Lake University's general education competence program is based on six General Education Competences which the university believes are characteristic of the liberally educated person. Graduates of Our Lady of the Lake University:

1. Have developed effective communication skills.
2. Have acquired sufficient understanding of their ever-changing physical environment to cope effectively with it and make responsible and intelligent judgments about it.
3. Have attained reflective and critical perspectives relative to their personal and interpersonal growth and the impact of culture and social institutions on human behavior.
4. Have achieved a reasoned, integrated understanding of the religious and ethical dimensions of human experience, both personal and social.
5. Have developed the ability to percieve and discriminate among artistic elements of their own and other cultures, and to describe and use their own creative processes.
6. Have acquired an understanding of basic synoptic theories, have developed effective synoptic skills, and can apply these skills in formulating their world views.

The six general competence statements are broken down into components and subcomponents intended to provide more direction to each competence statement. For example, the components of the third competence are:

1. Understand selected theories of development of the person; explain behaviors in terms of these theories; and apply these theories to the development of the self.
2. Understand selected theories related to interpersonal communication; describe social interactions in terms of these theories; and apply these theories in one's own personal interactions.
3. Understand the influence of culture on human behavior; explain behaviors within cultural contexts; and apply cultural

78

perspectives to self.
4. Within selected cultural contexts, understand the nature and development of social institutions; explain the relationships between individuals and social institutions; and estimate the potential for change within those relationships.

A competence "team," composed primarily of elected faculty members, has been set up for each of the six areas. The teams are responsible for seeing that evaluation procedures for the competences are observed, and for specifying the criteria by which students' competence will be judged.

There have been two basic methods of validating competence developed over the past four years. In-course validations are achieved within a regular course context; successful completion of a course validates particular components of competence. If they feel they are already competent in a particular area, students may select external validations in certain competence areas. External validations may include national examinations (e.g., CLEP examinations), though students are frequently assessed by three evaluators designated by the competence team. The assessment methods employed by evaluation teams range from written examinations and reports to journals and portfolios. As of this writing, other external validation methods are still being developed. To spell out what students must know and be able to do to complete the general education program, the university has drafted a document of general education requirements; this booklet describes the six general education competences in detail, suggests tasks or learning experiences for the student, and clearly explicates standards and means of validation.

The Our Lady of the Lake general education program has been designed in line with the general competence strategy of specifying learning objectives and designing an evaluation system and criteria before developing instructional strategies. The basic position adopted at the University was that "instructors should know what competences their courses are supposed to lead to before they are asked to design the courses and specify course objectives."

Within the last several years, faculty have redesigned courses and learning experiences and adopted two major new programs in response to the general education competences. A mentor program

79

provides each freshman with two mentors, a faculty
member and a sophomore or junior student, who work
with the student beginning with the August orientation. The mentor pair is responsible for seventeen
to twenty students in a group that continues to
meet during the academic year as the Personal
Development Seminar. The academic and personal
development of each student is assessed in the seminar and corrective work is prescribed for students
with problems. In addition, a major thrust of the
academic portion of the seminar is the study in
depth of a particular problem or research question
in the faculty mentor's area of expertise.

The change of emphasis at Our Lady of the Lake
University from a few tightly defined required
course sequences to learning results achieved
through alternative learning activities--including
credit by examination, experiential learning, and
other nontraditional evaluation techniques--has led
to the establishment of two major academic support
systems. An Assessment Center is in operation to
assist in the evaluation process, develop assessment instruments, and maintain records. An
expanded Learning Center has also become an important resource for students in a number of academic
areas.

Our Lady of the Lake has become a leader in
the competence-based movement. In 1977 it established a quarterly publication designed to provide
current information on competence learning to the
national postsecondary education community. A
variety of additional nationwide activities suggests the growth of the movement across the country.
In addition to numerous workshops and institutes, a
number of efforts have focused on the assessment of
competence. For example, the College Outcomes
Measures Project (COMP) has been organized by the
American College Testing Program to develop measurement devices and procedures to assess general education knowledge and skills. From all indications,
there is widespread interest in developing
competence-based programs of general education.

Although Brigham Young does not identify its
new general education program as competence-based,
those interested in one application of this
approach within a large university setting are
referred to the new general education program at
this university. BYU's university-wide program is
based on the guiding principle of competence-based
programs: "demonstration of mastery, not mere
attendance in classes, should lie behind the

University's certifying students' completion of GE requirements."

While competence-based programs have achieved a certain notoriety in academic circles, some harsh criticisms have been directed at them. The major criticism has been that in redefining education in terms of competence and in trying to measure the behavior that demonstrates competence, education is being reduced to a mechanistic measuring of specific behaviors. Especially in general education, where it is nearly impossible to measure a liberally educated person, the trend may lead to trivialization instead of true liberal learning.

Another criticism of these programs concerns changing faculty roles. "An entirely new concept of what a faculty member is requires different bases of training, recruitment, time, and evaluation for faculty members. Some faculty may not adjust, which means that, as one college put it, they will have to be 'physically separated' from the institution [Trivett, 1975, p. 62]."

If the detractors of competence-based programs are vociferous, it is also true that a substantial number of academics involved in curriculum planning take a more moderate if still skeptical view. For example, Russell Edgerton, the former deputy director of the Fund for the Improvement of Postsecondary Education, states that competence-based education is

. . . one of the most exciting--and most dangerous--things in American education today. We must ask ourselves whether this is another academic relabeling exercise, the purpose of which is to throw old practices into new robes; or worse, whether it will further increase the mechanization and bureaucratization of teaching, learning, and assessment [Chronicle of Higher Education, February 3, 1975 p. 1].

In spite of these concerns, a number of institutions have begun to implement competence-based general education programs. Whether these programs are viewed as exciting new innovations, a device for attracting attention, or worse, a way of undermining the serendipitous effects of general learning, it is clear that a large dose of idealism has given impetus to the development of this approach. Dissatisfaction with the slippery standards of normative evaluation, concern with new types of students, and a genuine desire to put the rhetoric of

81

general education into practice are often major reasons for beginning competence-based general education programs. In spite of the reservations about the latter, they are likely to survive in the indefinite future.

Freshman Seminars

Paralleling the development of interdisciplinary programs, many colleges and universities have adopted seminars or colloquia during the freshman year. These programs seek to provide students with an in-depth experience at the beginning of their college careers, in contrast to the large-size, broad, survey-type courses which frequently confront freshmen.

Colleges have long experimented with new approaches to teaching freshmen. For example, Lawrence University established a course called Freshman Studies in 1945. Nearly two decades later, Harvard adopted freshman seminars to provide an opportunity for outstanding students to meet for a semester with Harvard's greatest minds. The Harvard program was soon changed through the inclusion of a broad cross section of Harvard students and faculty. Today, most programs provide an opportunity for all freshmen to work with a faculty member in a small group on a topic of mutual interest.

Colleges and universities now use freshman seminars in a variety of ways: some include the seminars in the core curriculum; a few still reserve them exclusively for honors students; and still others use them as part of an orientation program. Yet this diversity should not obscure the common bond between the programs: most of them are designed to provide integrative, interdisciplinary, in-depth experiences for students beginning their collegiate experience.

A recent study of undergraduate education concluded that the "freshman seminar is today the most popular, fastest-growing structure in freshman education [Levine and Weingart, 1973, p. 29]." The popularity of this approach is reflected in the wide range of institutions that have adopted freshman seminars: Purdue University, Trinity College, University of Pittsburgh, Morningside College, University of Pennsylvania, and Amherst College.

Many institutions typically offer freshman seminars on a variety of topics. For example, students at Lewis and Clark College in Oregon are required to take at least one freshman seminar as part of the general studies requirement for graduation. Frequent meetings and classes limited to twenty students are designed to encourage development of confidence and skill in analyzing, making judgments, writing, and speaking. Because the particular expertise and enthusiasm of the instructor determine specific seminar subjects, the range of topics reflects the diversity of the faculty. Recent program offerings have included Symbiosis; the American West: Man and Nature; Gaming: A Cross-Disciplinary Approach; Futurology; and Literature and Revolution in Latin America.

The Freshman Seminars at Haverford College, consisting of the Freshman Seminar Program and the Freshman Writing Program, are required of all freshmen. For his first semester each freshman is assigned either to the seminar program or to a section of the Freshman Writing Seminar; in the second semester, the assignments are reversed.

The Freshman Seminar Program is intended to give the student a unique educational experience at the beginning of his college career. Taught by members of all divisions of the college, the seminars are interdisciplinary in approach rather than formal introductions to the various departments. Normally limited to fourteen students, each seminar meets regularly in two forms: as a group for the discussion of assigned readings, and in tutorials of three or four students each for the reading and criticism of papers. The seminars aim to encourage judicious reading, rigorous discussion, and effective writing, all in relation to coherently defined topics.

A student in the Freshman Seminar Program is placed in the seminar of his choice if it is compatible with the limitation on class size. The topics considered represent broad areas which are chosen to meet a variety of student intellectual interests and to combine the instructor's own concerns with this expertise. The topics and faculty change each year. Examples of topics offered in past seminars include Comparative Mythology: Uses of the Imagination; The Stalin Purges and Soviet Literature; Utopias and Communal Societies; The Self; The Scientist as Revolutionary; and Arthurian Literature and Music.

The Freshman Writing Seminar is designed to give freshmen an intensive experience in reading and writing on human values. Twice weekly class discussions are combined with tutorials of four or five students which are devoted to the detailed examination of student papers. Thus, the course combines an experience similar to that of the Freshman Seminar with additional training in written work which will serve the student during his academic career and beyond.

The courses offered in the writing seminar are diverse, giving the student an opportunity to explore an area new to him or to develop an interest he may already have. Two of the courses available, for example, are "Tragic and Comic Modes" and "On Reaching Others: Classical and Modern Rhetoric." Instructors represent various academic disciplines, although they come primarily from the English Department.

In a study of undergraduate education, two researchers examined the curricula of twenty-six liberal arts colleges. After intensively reviewing freshman seminar programs at six institutions, they found that student and faculty opinion of the seminars was generally positive. At the same time, they identified four major problems that were mentioned in most of the programs: the course is above the freshman level; the instructor is conducting a lecture course rather than a seminar; the course lacks content; and freshmen are often too shy to participate fully (Levine and Weingart, 1973, p. 30). While these and other potential problems deserve serious consideration, they do not negate the fact that the freshman seminar is the major innovation in freshman education. Like the other innovative approaches to general education, the freshman seminar represents an attempt to provide integrated and cohesive learning experiences for students.

APPLYING THE ORGANIZING PRINCIPLES TO PLANNING FOR
   GENERAL EDUCATION

Faced with such a bewildering array of curricular trends and innovations, how do curriculum planners integrate these developments into a framework for planning their particular general education program? First, they can apply the framework developed in the second chapter as a tool for analyzing their existing curriculum; using this method, they can attempt to determine the foundations and emphases of their existing programs. Second, they can analyze curricular innovations from other

84

institutions and determine how these innovations
suggest different ways of organizing general education. In this manner, the model becomes a useful
tool for conceptually organizing new innovations
instead of viewing them as separate entities, and
forcing curriculum planners to think in systemic
terms. Throughout this process, planners are con-
tinually asking the question: How do these innovations depart from existing curricular arrangements
and, if they are attractive, which innovations fit
together in a coherent curricular package? Third,
and before making any decisions about the general
education program, curriculum planners can use the
model to devise potential combinations of organizing principles and emphases not previously considered in organizing the curriculum.

After having analyzed the existing curriculum,
looked at a variety of innovations and their implications for new ways of organizing general education, and considered alternative ways of organizing
the program, curriculum planners are in a position
to propose an integrated plan. Throughout the planning process, the model can become an active
vehicle for planning changes in general education.

To illustrate the planning process, let us
assume that the curriculum committee at a hypothet-
ical institution is charged by the faculty senate
with the reexamination of the general education
program and, if necessary, the recommendation of
curricular modifications. Employing the model as a
device for analyzing the existing general education
program, the curriculum committee concludes that
the current program is organized around the academic disciplines. In addition to several basic
courses in foreign language and English composition,
students satisfy their general education requirements by taking thirty hours from among groups of
courses in the social sciences, natural sciences,
and the humanities--courses aimed at achieving
breadth in the students' program.

In analyzing the general education program in
terms of curricular emphases, it is obvious that
the current program is quite traditional in relation to the four continua outlined in the model.
The locus of learning is the campus-based classroom,
with no emphasis on experiential learning.
Moreover, the content of the curriculum reflects an
emphasis on breadth rather than depth, and the program is designed entirely by faculty. Finally, the
general education program is neither flexible nor
rigid; students have only a few required courses,

satisfying their requirements primarily through distribution. After analyzing the general education program in terms of both organizing principles and curricular emphases, the curriculum committee has a better conceptual understanding of the current organization of the program.

Turning its attention to recent curriculum developments in general education, the committee begins to employ the framework to analyze recent innovations in general education. First, members of the committee note that several recent changes are based on alternative organizing principles. For example, the general education program at Our Lady of the Lake University is competence-based. After finding examples of general education programs that are based on all five of the organizing principles, the committee then looks at the extent to which several innovations reflect curricular emphases different from those of their own institution. In terms of curricular content, for example, many of the recent innovations emphasize depth as well as breadth in the general education program. The freshman seminar, which has recently become popular, is a good example. In contrast to their own curriculum, several of the innovations emphasize student and contractually designed general education programs.

After the committee relates many of the innovations to its curriculum model, it attempts to imagine different general education programs which will reflect new combinations of organizing principles and curricular emphases that are not being emphasized at its institution or, to the best of its knowledge, elsewhere. A philosophy professor, who has spent several years working for the federal government, suggests that one new combination might be to wed the social problems organizing principle to experiential learning, and to organize the liberal education program accordingly. While there is a sharp initial reaction among committee members against incorporating the combination in their recommendations, there is agreement that the committee ought to at least entertain the idea. After several other members suggest some alternative combinations of organizing principles and curricular emphases, there is agreement that this use of the model-- which had earlier seemed hopelessly academic--has provoked the committee to think beyond existing curricula but within the context of an organizing framework.

After analyzing the existing curriculum,

looking at various innovations, and attempting to
generate new conceptions of general education--all
in terms of the curricular framework--the curriculum committee begins to think seriously about the
kinds of changes, if any, it might recommend. At
this juncture, the model again becomes a useful
tool as the committee moves from organizing principles and curricular emphases to proposing structural changes in the curriculum. Of course, there
is a substantial amount of disagreement before any
decisions are made, but as it begins the task of
making recommendations, the committee has at least
agreed that the model has been helpful in formulating an integrated and systemic curricular revision
for proposal to the faculty senate.

REFERENCES

Bell, Daniel. The Reforming of General Education.
    New York: Columbia University Press, 1966.
Ben-David, Joseph. American Higher Education:
    Directions Old and New. New York: McGraw-Hill,
    1972.
Bird, Caroline. The Case against College. New
    York: Bantam Books, 1975.
Blackburn, Robert, Ellen Armstrong, Clifton Conrad,
    James Didham, and Thomas McKune. Changing
    Practices in Undergraduate Education.
    Berkeley, California: Carnegie Council on
    Policy Studies in Higher Education, 1976.
Blackman, Edward. "General Education." In
    Robert L. Ebel (ed.), Encyclopedia of
    Educational Research. 4th ed. New York:
    Macmillan, 1969: 522-537.
Brick, Michael, and Earl J. McGrath. Innovations
    in Liberal Arts Colleges. New York: Teachers
    College Press, Columbia University, 1969.
Brubacher, John S., and Willis Rudy. Higher
    Education in Transition. 3rd ed. New York:
    Harper and Row, 1976.
The Carnegie Foundation for the Advancement of
    Teaching. Missions of the College Curriculum.
    San Francisco: Jossey-Bass, 1977.
Dressel, Paul L., and Frances H. DeLisle.
    Undergraduate Curriculum Trends. Washington,
    D.C.: American Council on Education, 1969.
Earnest, Ernest. Academic Procession: An Informal
    History of the American College. Indianapolis,
    Indiana: Bobbs-Merrill, 1953.

Freeman, Richard, and J. Herbert Hollomon. "The
     Declining Value of College Going." Change, 7
     (1975): 24-31, 62.
General Education in a Free Society: Report of the
     Harvard Committee. Cambridge, Massachusetts:
     Harvard University Press, 1945.
Hofstadter, Richard, and Wilson Smith (eds.).
     American Higher Education: A Documentary
     History. Volume II. Chicago: University of
     Chicago Press, 1961.
Levine, Arthur, and John Weingart. Reform of
     Undergraduate Education. San Francisco:
     Jossey-Bass, 1973.
McGrath, Earl. General Education and the Plight of
     Modern Man. Indianapolis, Indiana: Lilly
     Endowment, 1976.
O'Toole, James. "The Reserve Army of the
     Underemployed." Change, 7 (1975): 26-33.
Rudolph, Frederick. The American College and
     University: A History. New York: Vintage,
     1962.
Rudolph, Frederick. Curriculum: A History of the
     American Undergraduate Course of Study Since
     1636. San Francisco: Jossey-Bass, 1977.
Schmidt, George P. The Liberal Arts College. New
     Brunswick, New Jersey: Rutgers University
     Press, 1957.
Trivett, David A. Competency Programs in Higher
     Education. ERIC/Higher Education Research
     Report No. 7. Washington, D.C.: American
     Association for Higher Education, 1975.
Veysey, Laurence R. The Emergence of the American
     University. Chicago: University of Chicago
     Press, 1965.

4
Concentration

As it has developed since the Middle Ages,
liberal education has come to include the dual
dimensions of breadth and depth. In the twentieth
century these dimensions have been operationalized
in the American undergraduate curriculum as general
education and specialization or concentration. In
spite of this dual orientation of liberal education,
the breadth or general education dimension has
received most of the attention. The substance and
tone of the recent higher education literature
often gives one the impression that general education is the essential aspect of liberal education.
Indeed, if the major or concentration is mentioned
in a discussion of undergraduate education, it is
usually criticized for its unwarranted domination
of the curriculum. As Arthur Levine and John
Weingart (1973) note:

> With the gradual dilution of general education,
> concentration has become the prime focus of
> the undergraduate college. As the process of
> dilution occurred, the first two years of col-
> lege education lost their purpose. And when
> no substitute was offered, it was only natural
> that, by default, concentration filled the gap,
> since colleges are organized and faculty are
> trained according to speciality. But natural
> or not, the unfortunate result is that addi-
> tional specialization has been substitution
> for a failing breadth program [p. 64].

Although Levine and Weingart admit that the
emphasis on concentration has lessened somewhat,
their statement is typical of the blame placed on
the overspecialized major for the failure of undergraduate education in general and liberal education

in particular. D. Richard Little, for example, suggests that "the idea of the major dominates American higher education so completely that it has all but eliminated any genuine program of general or liberal education [Little, 1974, p. 99]." Daniel Bell (1966) notes this same trend in reference to Columbia College:

> The introduction of the major system, more than any other single element, changed the character of Columbia College in the last decade. While the trends were evident before the introduction of the change, the major system, by encouraging students (in some instances such as the sciences, by requiring them) to begin their majors in their sophomore or even freshman years, has fractured the "unity" of the lower college, with its emphasis on a common-core program [pp. 197-198].

Yet many who take a skeptical view also defend the case for specialization or concentration. Lewis Mayhew and Patrick Ford state that most students probably benefit from some concentrated work in a limited area "if only for the sake of seeing just how complex a single field is [Mayhew and Ford, 1971, p. 161]."

In spite of the controversy, concentration or specialization has been and undoubtably will remain an essential component of the undergraduate curriculum. Viewing it negatively and neglecting to consider its relationship to the purposes of undergraduate education often leads to a situation in which general education and specialization are posited as antithetical rather than complementary. Indeed, if undergraduate education has failed, perhaps it is due to this perceived conflict between its two essential dimensions rather than to the dominance of specialization:

> Unification of the liberal and specialized curricula must be achieved if a university is effectively to help a student obtain an education that frees him from subjects, departments, and egocentric fragmentation. A liberal education is possible only when a general and a specialized education complement one another, only when the particular perfects the general in both approach and purpose [Sturner, 1973, p. 158].

90

While concentration is surrounded by controversy, it is also an area in which many institutions are experimenting with new forms. The main
purpose of this chapter is to acquaint the reader
with the variety of innovative approaches to concentration. Three new arrangements for concentra-
tion--interdisciplinary majors, student-designed
majors, and career-oriented majors--will be examined in detail, including examples and discussion
of the strengths and weaknesses of the various
approaches. As an introduction, a brief historical
sketch and an examination of recent trends will
precede the discussion of innovative approaches. A
concluding section examines three important issues
that should be addressed by those involved in planning for concentration.

HISTORICAL ANTECEDENTS

The earliest use of the terms "major" and
"minor" was in the Johns Hopkins University
Register for the year 1877-78 (Dressel, 1963, p. 6).
The concept of the major did not become widespread,
however, until after the turn of the century. Its
acceptance was due in part to the changes which
Abbott Lawrence Lowell introduced at Harvard when
he became president in 1909. Reacting to the free
elective system developed by his predecessor,
Charles Eliot, Lowell established a system of concentration and distribution. In the freshman and
sophomore years students were required to choose
courses from groups of subjects, with each group
representing a wide range of related knowledge.
For the upper two years students picked a more
narrow field or department of concentration in
which they were required to take six full-year
courses. Lowell expressed his philosophy for this
system of concentration and distribution in his
inaugural address, stating that the ideal college

> . . . ought to produce, not defective special-
> ists, but men intellectually well rounded, of
> wide sympathies and unfettered judgment. At
> the same time they ought to be trained to hard
> and accurate thought and this will not come
> merely by surveying the elementary principles
> of many subjects. It requires mastery of
> something, acquired by continuous applica-
> tion . . . . The best type of liberal educa-
> tion in our complex and modern world aims at

producing men who know a little of everything and something well [Schmidt, 1957, p. 209].

Like the general education movement, the introduction of the major can be viewed as a reaction to the elective system of the later nineteenth century. It is perhaps more than coincidental that the major appeared at the same time that the faculty in American colleges and universities were becoming identified with individual disciplines. For with the growth of discipline-based professional organizations in the late nineteenth and early twentieth centuries, faculty identification with specialties became stronger and the curricula of institutions were soon organized into subject areas reflected in departmental structures.

The major has also been an important mechanism for adaptation in the college curriculum during the twentieth century. It was a vehicle for introducing the new knowledge that was generated by scientific and humanistic inquiry beginning at the turn of the century. In addition, it served the purpose of training students at a level of specialization that was appropriate for entry into occupational fields that did not always require more advanced graduate training. As the graduate schools developed after World War II, there was also increased pressure from above to prepare undergraduate students in the disciplines.

Nurtured by departmental interests and student concerns about the relationship between education and occupational choice, the major has become a central component of the undergraduate experience. Yet if concentration has recently enjoyed far more success than programs of general education, traditional patterns of concentration have also been subjected to scrutiny. The bulk of this chapter will document recent efforts to modify concentration patterns in ways that offer alternative conceptions of specialization and threaten the domination of departments over concentration.

RECENT TRENDS IN CONCENTRATION

Within the last decade, there have been several major studies of the undergraduate major or concentration. In a study of undergraduate curricular trends in the late 1960s, Paul Dressel and Frances DeLisle (1969) collected data from 322 institutions. They summarize their findings on the

92

major concentration in three statements:

1. The departmental major remains the most common pattern, but there is evident an increase in the use of broader theme, area, divisional, or interdepartmental approaches.
2. Major requirements are supplemented by cognate or related course requirements in some 60 percent of the institutions, but there has been some decrease in the amount and in the specification of such requirements.
3. There is great variation in the concentration or major requirements although the modal practice remains at 24 to 32 credits or 8 courses [p. 32].

Dressel and DeLisle note that one of the difficulties in researching the major is that there are so many different concepts of what constitutes a major. The place of introductory courses and the inclusion or exclusion of "directed electives" are only two of the factors that affect the definition of a major. The researchers found that the concepts of depth and sequence were most commonly invoked as guides to planning for the major concentration and that the accumulation of specified courses and credits were the basic underlying rationale for the major (Dressel and DeLisle, 1969, pp. 32-33).

A recent study sponsored by the Carnegie Council on Policy Studies in Higher Education examined changes in the undergraduate curriculum between 1967 and 1974 at 210 colleges and universities. In analyzing trends in the undergraduate major, the researchers selected six majors for intensive analysis: English, philosophy, biology, physics, political science, and psychology. The researchers found that between 1967 and 1974 there was essentially no change in the number of courses individual majors require and in the fraction of the total degree requirement represented by a major. They further concluded, on the basis of an examination of student course-taking patterns at ten selected institutions, that "regardless of whether an institution had otherwise changed its curriculum, little has been altered in the amount of course work required or taken to complete a major [Blackburn, Armstrong, Conrad, Didham, and McKune, 1976, p. 34]."

The researchers in this study also found that as the number of electives a student could take had increased over the seven-year period, many of these electives were taken in the division of specialization: natural sciences, social sciences, or humanities. They concluded that in institutions where the percentage of electives available to students has increased, the greatest share of the electives is being used to achieve more depth in undergraduate studies. As they put it: "The overall course-taking pattern for the degree shows a significant increase in depth and a corresponding diminution of breadth [p. 35]." Thus, although the formal major requirements of a college may demand no more than a third of a student's time in some fields, the fact is that many students use substantial portions of their electives to intensify specialization beyond that which is required, in effect increasing the proportion of their program actually used for the major. Undergraduate concentration has become the dominant feature of the undergraduate experience.

NEW ARRANGEMENTS FOR CONCENTRATION

Postsecondary institutions today are acutely aware of their need to examine the place of the undergraduate major. Certain external and internal pressures have been instrumental in bringing about this sensitivity. Among them is the significant change in the clientele of postsecondary education. Not only are more people attending educational institutions after high school, but they are distributed among the various socioeconomic strata in a different pattern than in previous years. This fact has implications for institutions evaluating their major program, as Charles Stanton (1976) observes:

> During the past decade the clientele of American higher education has altered considerably. In the past those drawn to colleges and universities represented the upper socioeconomic classes, but in recent years an entirely new stratum of American society has sought and attained access to higher learning. The children of blue collar workers and laborers--the first in their families to attend college--now flood campuses. They perceive higher learning as the means to a higher

94

status occupation and increased earnings.
Whereas the sons and daughters of professional
and successful business men sought acceptance
in the upper strata of society, with its
demand for at least a brush with the high culture, the children from the working classes
now desire occupational mobility [p. 299].

This changing clientele, with its higher
career aspirations, confronts a society in which
occupational opportunity and mobility are considerably less than they were a decade ago. Most of
these students seek areas of specialization that
will lead to an attractive job. Institutions also
experience certain internal pressures for change.
Increasing departmental specialization and growth
during the 1960s resulted in a large and relatively
autonomous faculty in many institutions. As students enrolling in institutions changed their orientation, many traditional departments were confronted
with a question to which they were ill-equipped to
respond: What can I do with an undergraduate major
in this field? Among many others, departments of
history and foreign languages found their enrollments sharply declining.
As a consequence of these developments, many
postsecondary institutions have introduced a variety
of new programs of specialization or concentration.
For example, some schools have introduced double,
joint, and interdepartmental majors. While there
are many new variations of concentration, most of
the innovations in concentration can be grouped
under three broad categories: interdisciplinary
majors, student-designed majors, and career-
oriented majors.

Interdisciplinary Majors

Interdisciplinary majors have increased markedly in popularity during the past several years.
A recent study by the Carnegie Council on Policy
Studies in Higher Education found that the interdisciplinary major was the most prevalent alternative to traditional majors; 79 percent of the colleges of arts and sciences in the 270 institutions
studied offered interdisciplinary majors (The
Carnegie Foundation for the Advancement of Teaching,
1977, p. 193).
Like interdisciplinary general education programs, the common denominator of the interdisciplinary majors is a focus on a problem, theme, or

issue which cuts across two or more academic disciplines. More than any other component of the undergraduate curriculum, these programs are emerging in idiosyncratic ways on campus: the forms that they take are a function of the beliefs, energies, and predilections of the persons promoting them, and of the character of the institution and the supporting community.

Because these programs draw upon the particular human and physical resources of each institution, a seemingly endless variety of interdisciplinary majors has been adopted throughout the country. In one large university, for example, as many as thirty interdisciplinary majors are available to students. Some of these majors are psychobiology, sociolinguistics, medieval study, and area studies (e.g., African Studies). Although the variety of new interdisciplinary majors is almost bewildering, many institutions offer interdisciplinary majors in related topical areas which deserve special consideration. These interdisciplinary programs can be broken down into four separate groupings: environmental studies, women's studies, ethnic studies, and urban studies.

Environmental Studies Majors. Perhaps the most well-known of the new interdisciplinary majors, this field has grown rapidly because of society's interest in providing protection and control over the quality of man's environment. Environmental studies majors draw upon such diverse disciplines as management science, engineering, water and soil conservation, chemistry, biology, architecture, and a host of other disciplines that often seem only tangentially related. There is considerable diversity in many of the new environmental studies majors. Most important, some of the new programs emphasize the scientific aspects of ecological problems while others combine studies of the environment with the study of man.

An interesting example of this new type of major is the Environmental Studies Program at Sweet Briar College. One of the outstanding features of the multidisciplinary Environmental Studies Program at Sweet Briar is the Coordinate Major. The Coordinate program enables a student majoring in any discipline to coordinate her major with the human ecology emphasis in environmental studies. A student could, for example, major in English, art history, anthropology, or physics, and in each case coordinate her major with the Environmental Studies

Program.

At the end of their sophomore year, students meet with the chairman of their department and the Environmental Studies Coordinator to plan their academic program. There are three main requirements in the program: a core course in environmental studies, an independent study project, and the Senior Seminar. The most prominent interdisciplinary feature of the program is the core course, entitled "The Environment: What Are Man's Choices?," in which professors from about a dozen different departments focus their respective disciplines on environmental concepts. The course is divided into six sections, each of which has a common theme. The course is united by a fifty-five page syllabus reflecting a carefully integrated interdisciplinary approach to environmental studies. The section topics include The Natural Sciences and the Environment, Environmental Economics, Environmental Politics, and Ethics and Aesthetics.

The second requirement is that students carry out an independent study project on any environmental topic that interests them and is approved by their advisors. Finally, there is the Senior Seminar. While this can follow any number of formats, its major purpose is to allow Coordinate Majors in their last year an opportunity to pursue topics of special interest--selected by common agreement--in considerable depth under the guidance of an expert.

One additional type of activity available to students is the applied environmental research performed for local agencies by both student and faculty investigators. An example of this is a contract with a local pulp mill which called for a three-year survey of the biology and chemistry of a twenty-mile stretch of the James River near the College. Students work both in the field and in the laboratory for course credit or pay, depending on the nature of the task. While these are only the main features of Sweet Briar's Environmental Studies Program, they suggest one way of adapting such a program to institutional and community resources while maintaining a concerted interdisciplinary thrust.

Women's Studies Majors. From only two programs in 1970, the number of women's studies programs has grown to 112 in 1974 and 270 in early 1977 (Howe, 1977, p. 15). Many of these programs offer students opportunities for concentration

either through dual majors, interdisciplinary concentrations related to career goals, or both. The
major impetus for these programs has been the
efforts of women to achieve equality and personal
freedom in education and American society by offering an alternative to the male-centered curriculum.
Most of these majors have an interdisciplinary
focus through the study of problems which cut
across traditional disciplines: the status of women
in history, comparative sex roles, the socialization process, and a variety of other contemporary
issues such as the roles and lifestyles of contemporary women in education, politics, medicine, and
science.*

One of the most well-known of these programs is
the Women's Studies Program at the University of
Pennsylvania. Women's Studies at Penn is an interdisciplinary program which offers all students an
opportunity to learn about the history and present
condition of women. Emphasis in the program is on
research--on discovering information, generating
questions, and creating innovative strategies for
understanding and changing lives. Toward that end,
most of the classes are informally structured.
Students are encouraged to engage in original work
which will make a contribution to the collective
understanding of women. Students have explored
such diverse topics as women in the whaling industry, adultery in the twentieth-century American
novel, women patent holders in the nineteenth century, the sex-role socialization of preschool children in West Philadelphia, cross-cultural views of
menstruation, and the oral history of surviving
women who took part in the suffrage struggle.

Women's Studies is a flexible academic program
within the Faculty of Arts and Sciences (FAS). The
curriculum consists of approximately two dozen day-
and evening-school courses offered by traditional
FAS departments, plus a cluster of four themati-
cally interrelated upper-level seminars. The clus-
ters of thematically-related seminars are designed
to give students a multidisciplinary understanding

_____

*An excellent review of the current state of
Women's Studies in a selected number of colleges
and universities is A Report of the National
Advisory Council on Women's Educational Programs.
See Howe, 1977.

of a particular problem concerning women. "Women and Power" was the topic through the 1977-78 academic year.

Students choosing to major in Women's Studies design an individualized major proposal with the help of the coordinator and another advisor. There are three steps to working out a major proposal. The first is thinking about the intellectual and vocational needs the student wishes to satisfy. The second is choosing twelve central courses (including two or three independent study or field work projects) and a group of related courses that are relevant to those interests. The third is writing a short essay stating the student's particular concerns and explaining how the proposed combination of courses is related to those concerns. If the advisor endorses the proposal, it is usually accepted by the Committee on Individualized Majors.

An important part of the Women's Studies Program at Penn takes place outside of classrooms. The program sponsors informal student-faculty dinners, speakers, conferences, and community-oriented workshops. In addition, the program cooperates with other campus organizations to help ensure that Penn provides all of its students with a learning environment which strongly supports women.

Ethnic Studies Majors. According to one researcher, approximately two-thirds of the nation's colleges and universities have adopted courses or programs in the relatively new field of ethnic studies (Heiss, 1973, p. 86). The underlying purpose of intensive study in these programs is to encourage the understanding of and appreciation for the cultural, intellectual, social, and economic contributions of various minorities. Three ethnic studies programs in particular have experienced rapid growth in the past several years: Black Studies, Mexican-American Studies, and Native American Studies.

The major aim of new programs in Black or Afro-American Studies has been to provide background courses on the history, art, music, and cultural characteristics of black people. In a number of programs, the curriculum has also been designed to prepare students for careers in urban affairs, community agencies, social welfare, and a variety of people-oriented fields. Mexican-American or Chicano Studies programs have a strong interdisciplinary base in the social sciences; most of these programs involve a core of interdisciplinary courses on the contributions of Mexican-Americans to American society.

A number of colleges west of the Mississippi River have introduced majors in Native American Studies. Like the other ethnic studies programs, these majors focus on the contributions of the minority group in terms of art, music, culture, and history.

An interesting example of an ethnic studies major is the Afro-American Studies program at Yale University. The Program examines, from an inter-disciplinary perspective, the historical, cultural, and intellectual development of people of African descent in the New World. The student in Afro-American Studies is expected to acquire a large measure of analytical ability in a specified field, such as anthropology or psychology. The program is built on a rather unique approach to knowledge: the wide cross-disciplinary range of the subject brought to focus finally (in the junior and senior years) through the narrow lens of the discipline.

A Yale student may either major in Afro-American Studies with a concentration in a tradi-tional discipline or take a double major in Afro-American Studies and a traditional discipline. Thus each student must have an area of concentra-tion in one field such as anthropology, economics, English, folklore, history, music, political science, psychology, religion, or sociology. The major itself requires fourteen courses which form the core of the major and serve to introduce funda-mental questions in Afro-American Studies from various points of view. In addition, a series of specialized seminars allows the student to explore more fully questions arising from the core curric-ulum.

There are two noteworthy features of the Program: the Senior Essay and the Senior Colloquium. Early in the junior year each major in Afro-American Studies begins seriously considering a topic for a Senior Essay. The objective of the Senior Essay is to enable a student to collect and evaluate evidence relating to the black experience and to write a concise, fully documented report of his conclusions. The essay must meet the general standards for research in the student's major dis-cipline (e.g., in history a student is expected to concentrate on primary rather than secondary sources). The student must also demonstrate a clear knowledge of the general bibliography and methodology of his discipline and the relationship

100

of each to his area of interest in Afro-American Studies.

The Senior Colloquium provides an opportunity for majors to exchange ideas with accomplished scholars who, in turn, share with the students the results of their current research. This interchange attempts to build full intellectual freedom: older scholars critique the work of younger scholars, and students are free to challenge critically even the most authoritative pronouncements of their teachers. The senior's essay is open to constructive critical discussion at each stage of its evolution; the professor's ideas are open to what may prove to be creative and sometimes unorthodox questioning. Especially in its use of the Senior Essay and Senior Colloquium, the Yale major in Afro-American Studies is a rich example of an ethnic studies major.

Urban Studies Majors. Many colleges and universities are now offering interdisciplinary programs of concentration in urban studies. The main goal of such programs is to provide the student with a broad understanding of the problems of cities and their inhabitants. The programs often draw upon a variety of disciplines: the social sciences, environmental design, education, city planning, and criminology. In addition, they usually involve field work and utilize the resources of the community.

At the College of Wooster, located in Wooster, Ohio, an Urban Studies program provides an interdisciplinary major and an off-campus urban experience for both majors and nonmajors. Emphasizing primarily the social sciences, the Urban Studies program is sponsored by the departments of economics, political science, and sociology, and is administered by a faculty committee.

Within the major the student is required to take the introductory course in sociology and economics as well as the urban studies-related course in each of the three core departments (urban and regional economics, urban politics, and urban processes and change). In addition to two elective courses and a research methodology course selected from the three sponsoring departments, two other courses must be taken from the supporting departments, including religion, history, art, black studies, and biology. Satisfactory completion of an urban quarter, an Independent Study Thesis, and an interdisciplinary senior seminar comprise the

101

balance of the program.

The most distinctive feature of the Urban Studies program is the Urban Quarter, which provides ten-week field placements for both majors and nonmajors in Birmingham, Philadelphia, Portland, St. Louis, and San Diego. The Urban Quarter experience is characterized as neither a "laboratory" nor a "practicum"; instead, the program views the student as a "participant-observer" of the urban condition. While the Urban Quarter adds a different mode of learning to the mix of student experiences, particularly because of its emphasis on experiential learning, the Quarter is also designed to encourage an academic understanding of the city. The three stated goals of the Urban Quarter for Urban Studies majors reflect these emphases:

1. The Urban Quarter is to provide the student a first-hand experience of the city. As a result of this experience, the student should be able to distinguish cities from noncities experientially. The student should become acquainted with the nature and range of activities and interactions that occur in cities. He should become familiar with how the people of the city view it; he should become aware of the reasons people give for their actions and the actions of others. The student should become familiar with sources of utilitarian information, the kind of information useful in functioning effectively in the city.

2. The student should develop a conceptual understanding of the city and its elements. He should be able to encompass the activities he has witnessed in concepts. He should be able to identify political, social, economic, and other functions of the city. He should begin the development of questions about causes and consequences. He should become familiar with the sources of information that will allow such questions to be answered.

3. The student should develop a theoretical understanding of the city. He should be able to conceptualize the city as a system of vertical and horizontal interactions. He should understand the city as a legal, social, and economic entity. He should develop an appreciation for the external context of the city: both the horizontal

102

relationships with other cities (e.g.,
metropolitanism), and the vertical relationships with other social systems (e.g.,
state and national). He should develop an
understanding of the interrelatedness of
functions. He should acquire the more
sophisticated understanding that is provided by a theoretical approach, such as
"the general systems" approach [College
of Wooster, n.d.].

In its Urban Quarter, the College of Wooster has
developed a unique mixture of several features
noted earlier: an interdisciplinary orientation, a
focus on the broad understanding of the city, and
an emphasis on experiential learning.

This overall discussion of new interdisciplinary majors has been selective, yet is suggestive of
recent developments. For those who are considering
the pros and cons of interdisciplinary majors, it
is useful to summarize some of the main arguments.
Arguments against the establishment of separate
interdisciplinary majors are often voiced by those
most committed to the continued dominance of the
traditional discipline-based academic department.
It is frequently pointed out that departments,
which are based on well-established traditions for
organizing and communicating knowledge, are best
equipped to offer programs of concentration. The
usual companion to this argument is that interdisciplinary majors often lead to the creation of
second-class faculties and educational experiences.

More specifically, it is argued that offering
an integrated interdisciplinary program comprised
of faculty originally trained in traditional academic perspectives presents serious problems.
While this difficulty may not be insurmountable in
course offerings for which individual faculty
assume full responsibility, most programs attempt
to integrate their majors through one or more interdisciplinary seminars or experiences in which
several faculty approach the subject matter from
very different perspectives. As a consequence,
course and program integration may suffer if participating faculty are unable to transcend their own
perspectives, relating them to other viewpoints
throughout the course of student instruction. Of
course, this problem is likely to be most acute in
those programs where the faculty have at least
part-time appointments in an outside department.
Finally, and in a more practical vein, critics of

interdisciplinary programs cite the staffing and administrative costs of establishing new majors outside of existing departmental arrangements.

Proponents of interdisciplinary majors can point to a number of positive characterists of the programs. Perhaps most important, an interdisciplinary program often serves to focus attention on a field of knowledge which the existing departmental arrangements have long tended to ignore. A previously unavailable area of concentration is opened to students. Moreover, such a program can lead to increased interaction between the institution and the outside community serving as an educational agent, breaking down barriers in the process. Thus, by its very existence, a new program may promote awareness and lead to individual, institutional, and social change. In the process, students may be better able to relate their education to the outside world, both in terms of employment and in preparation for a future of lifelong learning.

Student-Designed Majors

According to a recent survey, roughly one-third of all colleges of arts and sciences now offer student-designed majors (The Carnegie Foundation for the Advancement of Teaching, 1977, p. 195). Of course, the primary impetus for these programs is the idea that students should be responsible for planning their own program of concentration. Usually in concert with a faculty member or faculty committee, a student identifies an area of interest and then outlines a course of study. A student's program may or may not be interdisciplinary, be related to his career interests, or involve regular participation in traditional classroom instruction. In short, his program of specialization may be as unique as he wishes to design it, as long as the institution is willing to grant credit for the program. Two institutions, Juniata College and the State University of New York at Binghamton (SUNY-Binghamton), have recently adopted student-designed majors.

Juniata College, located in Huntingdon, Pennsylvania, offers a Program of Emphasis or "student-designed major." Rejecting the idea of rigid requirements for specialization, the Juniata curriculum requires only that each student draft his own "program of emphasis," listing the "units" he intends to take and explaining how each of them will help him to achieve his educational and

vocational goals. The entire Juniata curriculum
and the "program of emphasis" are based on the
assumption that each student must decide for himself what he is trying to accomplish in college.

At Juniata the term "units" is used instead of
"courses," since students can earn credit in a
variety of other ways in addition to taking
traditionally-conducted lecture courses. For
example, a student can complete an independent
study or research project, spend a year abroad or
part of a year at another college, work on a one-to-
one "tutorial" basis with a faculty member, or
acquire practical experience through an internship
at a factory, business establishment, hospital or
with a social or governmental agency.

A student can design "units" himself and
receive credit for them if what he proposes is considered academically worthwhile. Students have
been participating in more innovative experiences
each year. Two women students each earned three
units by spending a term as volunteer workers and
observers at a psychiatric hospital. Two other
women visited elementary schools in several states
and wrote critiques of the educational goals and
methods employed at the schools. An art student
constructed a kiln at his home and opened a small
ceramics business.

A "program of emphasis" can be very innovative,
or it can be very traditional, consisting entirely
of classroom work. It can combine apparently
divergent fields (for example, a student preparing
for graduate study in medical illustrating combined
units in art, biological sciences, and the humanities), or it can concentrate heavily in a single
subject. In many cases the "program of emphasis"
will correspond to a traditional discipline or
speciality; however, "programs of emphasis" that
are constructed from the components of several
traditional disciplines have equal validity, as do
those that include units with no close relationship to traditional disciplines.

Each student must make his own educational
decisions and then justify his program in writing.
The written justification is submitted to a
faculty-student committee for approval and becomes
a part of the student's permanent academic record.
Every student selects two faculty members who serve
as his advisors and help him develop his program.

The basic requirement for a "program of emphasis" is that it consist of fifteen academically
justifiable and related units which will help the

student achieve the objectives he sets for himself at Juniata. Students draft tentative "programs of emphasis" in the middle of their freshman year. In the required Freshman Seminar course, students receive instruction in preparing the first draft of their program. They must have approval for ten of the required fifteen units by the end of their sophomore year and for all fifteen by the close of their junior year. These fifteen units become part of a total four-year program of thirty-six units. Students are not locked into their original proposals. They can make changes or submit an entirely new program at any time. In fact, most students eventually refine their initial plans. Especially in light of its flexibility, the Juniata "program of emphasis" represents an interesting application of the concept of a student-designed major.

The Innovational Projects Board (IPB), a standing committee of Harpur College, SUNY-Binghamton, acts as the agency of the Harpur governing body in approving proposals made by individual students for interdepartmental major programs not listed in the catalog. Composed of five faculty members, three students, and the Dean of Harpur College, the IPB is charged with facilitating "innovative" academic challenges within the Harpur College curriculum. Thus, in addition to considering proposals for student-designed majors, the IPB may also grant academic credit for innovative courses and individual or group study projects.

Generally, IPB majors combine courses from two or more departments (for example, a Genetics major might combine courses in biology, psychology, and anthropology). Sometimes a major is not only interdisciplinary but also has a particular point of view or central problem. For example, one IPB-approved major entitled "Transvaluation and Crisis in Post Industrial Society" combined courses in philosophy, sociology, political science, and psychology to examine social values and value change in the post-industrial world.

The IPB operates on the assumption that students pursuing liberal arts degrees should have a broad base for their studies. Therefore, a highly specific study (any study which is, in effect, a subfield in an established discipline) does not warrant IPB consideration. For instance, a proposal for an "Ethics" major would be viewed as a proposal to study a subfield of philosophy and therefore would not qualify; in the same way,

106

majors in painting (a subfield of art studio) or
cartography (a subfield of geography) would not
qualify.

For the IPB, a "broad base" also implies that
a student proposes to study those areas which,
although they are not directly related to the specific goals of the major, are prerequisite to the
study of the major field. For instance, while a
predance therapy major has its own specific goals,
a student with such a major should study psycho-
physiology (which has statistics as a prerequisite),
anatomy, and so on, in order to prepare for the
actual enterprise of dance therapy. Therefore, one
requirement of a predance therapy major would be
statistics, although, on the surface it seems unrelated.

The most noteworthy feature of the program is
the proposal for individual major programs, which
is also submitted to the IPB. This process begins
when the student secures a letter of endorsement
from a Harpur College faculty member. Since most
IPB majors are interdisciplinary, students often
have two faculty sponsors, with the primary sponsor
being the person from the field in which the majority of the work is to be done. The letter to the
IPB must show that the faculty sponsor knows the
student, has read the proposal, and endorses it.

The essential aspect of the proposal is a
statement or narrative prepared by the student
describing the objectives of the program and demonstrating that the choice of courses which form the
basis of the major program is consistent with the
objectives. The narrative explains why the student
has chosen this area and addresses the major in a
general way, perhaps explaining what broad divisions exist within it and what personal circum-
stances led to the designing of the major.

The actual listing and explanation of courses
comprising the major is the most important section
of the proposal. The last course listed is the
"integrative project." The purpose of the project
is to weave together the program's various strands
and to have the student examine in depth some area
of his major. Its content and structure depend
entirely on the individual major. If a student is
able to design a defensible proposal, a process
which usually includes a rewrite, then the chances
are good that the project will be accepted by the
IPB. Some of the recent titles of individual
majors, such as Pre-Dance Therapy or Women and the
American Experience, suggest that Harpur College's

107

Innovational Project Board is indeed facilitating academic innovation in undergraduate concentration at SUNY-Binghamton.

One advantage of student-designed majors, as suggested by the two preceding examples, is that through individualization of the major, students are often given considerable flexibility through the assumption of prime responsibility for planning their own programs. Instead of being confined to a relatively narrow set of departmental offerings, which seldom enable a student to approach a problem, theme, or issue from a variety of perspectives, he has the option of designing a program more suited to his own particular interests. In turn, student motivation for learning is probably enhanced as students become active participants in the shaping of their area of specialization. On the negative side, such programs are often criticized for reasons similar to those leveled at the establishment of new interdisciplinary majors: they are difficult to integrate effectively, time-consuming for faculty, costly to administer, and sometimes inadequate preparation for graduate school.

Career-Oriented Majors

Career-oriented majors comprise the third new arrangement for concentration. While many of these programs are interdisciplinary in orientation, they are of sufficient importance to consider as a separate category. All career-oriented majors share the attempt to relate a student's specialization to the world of work. In most cases, an institution identifies a career area for which it does not offer preparation in its own programs. In turn, an existing department or group of departments offers a new major which is directly related to that career. In a few instances, a new department or academic unit is formed to administer the program.

Although career-oriented majors have become very popular in the past several years, there have been few studies of the new fields and, indeed, little information on them has been published other than a national listing of major fields of study. To fill this gap, I conducted a survey to find out more about these new majors, using a sample based upon the classification system developed by the Carnegie Commission on Higher Education (Carnegie,

1973, pp. 6-7).* The final sample included 114
institutions.

Letters were sent to the Dean of the College
of Liberal Arts and Sciences at each of the institutions. The letter requested that the Dean identify
new majors adopted at his institution since the fall
of 1972. Sixty-three institutions or 55 percent of
the sample, responded to the initial and follow-up
letters.

In classifying the various majors, a broad
definition of career-oriented majors was used:
areas of concentration which seem to bear a direct
relationship to the world of work.** Thus music
management or art therapy, both of which involve
preparation for work in those respective fields,
were considered career-oriented majors. On the
other hand, a new sociology major, if it was primarily oriented toward the preparation of social
scientists, was not classified as a career-oriented
major. While this kind of distinction was occasionally difficult to make, I chose to err on the side
of inclusiveness rather than commit various sins of

_____

*This schema generates five major institutional
categories: research universities, other doctoral-
granting universities, comprehensive universities
and colleges, liberal arts colleges, and community
colleges. The first four classes were each split
into two groups on a student-selectivity basis.
Each cell was then divided once again by type of
control (public or private) to produce sixteen categories. The alphabetical list of institutions in
each category was numbered consecutively and a table
of random numbers determined selection. The number
of institutions per category was determined by taking: 1) a 5 percent sample per Carnegie type,
except that each cell had to have no fewer than six
institutions; and 2) a 7.5 percent sample in the
three largest cells to capture their possible variety. The category including selective public
liberal arts institutions was dropped since there
were only two institutions in that category. The
final sample of 114 institutions was drawn from the
remaining fifteen categories.

**While some of these fields have been around for
many years, I was interested in the majors that
were new to the institutions sampled.

omission. At the same time, it is important to emphasize that this classification does not mean to imply that the career-oriented majors are something less than traditional liberal arts majors, for they are all offered within Colleges of Liberal Arts and Sciences. It would also be unfair and misleading to identify these majors with vocational education programs. Rather, many of the majors represent new syntheses of liberal and career or professional education.

Of the sixty-three institutions included in the sample, fifty-two have instituted at least one new career-oriented major since 1972. For purposes of analysis and because of the relatively low rate of response to the survey, the Carnegie classification system used for sampling was collapsed in order to make comparisons between institutional types (research universities, other doctoral-granting universities, comprehensive universities and colleges, and liberal arts colleges) and by type of control (public or independent). Comprehensive universities and colleges, such as the State University of New York at Brockport and the University of Evansville, were the most innovative institutions in terms of the absolute numbers of new majors. Partly because of the vigorous activity in the public comprehensive universities and colleges, public institutions adopted more new majors than independent institutions. Across the entire sample, however, differences by institutional type and type of control were not marked, and the general conclusion is that there has been an overall trend toward incorporating career-oriented majors in the undergraduate curriculum.

Roughly two-thirds of the new majors reported in the survey were classified as career-oriented. Figure 4.1 lists only the career-oriented majors reported by the sample institutions. (Majors reported by more than one institution are followed by parentheses indicating the number of schools which have adopted the new program.) An examination of the figure reveals that a number of new topic areas and individual majors are beginning to be included in undergraduate concentration offerings. The increasing number of new majors in health-related areas, recreation and leisure, technical areas such as computer science, and arts and law-related fields suggests that these areas are becoming especially popular. Within these broad areas, several individual majors have been adopted by more than one school: computer science, criminal justice and

FIGURE 4.1.   NEW CAREER-ORIENTED MAJORS

Agri-Business
Allied Health Sciences
Applied Mathematics-Economics
Applied Mathematics-Psychology
Art Therapy (2)
Arts and Sciences and Business
Arts for Children
Arts Management
Athletic Training

Behavioral Sciences and Health Care
Biological Technology
Biomedical Ethics

Coaching Athletics
Communication Studies (5)
Community Health
Community Health Education
Community Studies
Community Services (2)
Computer Science (12)
Contemporary Ministries
Criminal Justice (8)

Dance

Earth Science (2)
Equestrian Studies
Environmental Administration
Environmental Science (2)
Environmental Studies (3)

Forestry

Health Associate
Health Care Administration (2)
Health Education
Health Occupations Education
Health Studies
Hospital Administration
Hospital Finance Management
Hotel and Restaurant Management
Human Services

Industrial Arts
Industrial Chemistry and Management
Industrial Technology
International Business

111

Law and Justice
Law and Society
Law Enforcement
Law, Public Policy and Society
Legal Administration

Manpower Management
Medical Technology (3)
Music Management
Music Merchandising
Music Therapy (2)

Physician's Assistant
Police Science and Administration
Pre-Music Therapy
Public Administration (5)
Public Affairs

Recreation and Leisure (3)
Recreation Management
Rehabilitation
Respiration Therapy

Science Education For the Inner City
Sport Studies
Systems Management

Technical Communication
Telecommunications

Urban Administration
Urban Society
Urban Studies

Wildlife Management

law, communication studies, public administration, recreation and leisure, and environmental science and studies. Interestingly, over one-half of these new majors are interdisciplinary.

Before discussing specific examples of these new career-oriented majors, several serendipitous findings of the open-ended survey should be mentioned. Two trends in the responses indicate that in addition to creating new majors, institutions are also using other approaches to relate student concentration to occupational preparation. First, ten institutions in the sample have adopted career-oriented minors within at least one of their major departments in the College of Arts and Sciences. For example, the Asian Studies Program at Florida State University has established a special career-oriented minor in multinational business. Second, twenty-three of the schools in the sample have provisions for student-designed or individualized majors. Because these majors can have a career orientation, this type of major allows students to pursue various paths of concentration that may be directly related to their anticipated career choice to an extent unavailable in the existing curriculum. Therefore, in addition to establishing new career-oriented majors, there are at least two other ways in which institutions now foster new relationships between undergraduate concentration and the world of work: creating career-oriented minors within established departments and offering student-designed majors which give students the opportunity to design more work-related fields of concentration.

These two trends notwithstanding, most institutions have preferred to deal with work and education issues by establishing new career-oriented majors. To provide some sense of the structure of these new majors, several examples will be discussed briefly.

At the University of Utah, the College of Social and Behavioral Science has instituted a new major in Behavioral Sciences and Health leading to an Interdisciplinary Social Science Degree (Health Sciences). The program was begun at least in part because of a growing realization among faculty in the College that cross-disciplinary alternatives were needed to facilitate the application of basic knowledge to emerging problems in our society. In addition, there was the recognition of a growing need for behavioral scientists with a combination of methodological skills, administrative skills,

113

and a conceptual understanding of community health-related matters.

The Utah program attempts to combine a unique set of skills with a strong liberal education dimension. The core of the curriculum includes requirements in methodological skills, health care resources and administration, and theoretical and conceptual issues in health. The methodological skills requirement includes statistics and research methods drawn from courses in sociology, English, psychology, anthropology, geography, economics, and family and community medicine. Requirements in health care resources and administration include courses in the geography of health and health care, health sciences, and political science, as well as a twelve-hour practicum in a health-related agency. The last component of the core includes courses in philosophy (bio-ethics), sociology (medical sociology) and psychology (behavioral aspects of health) as well as a seminar on Health and Society. Instituted in the fall of 1977, the new major in the behavioral sciences and health includes several of the main characteristics of emerging programs of concentration: a career-orientation, an interdisciplinary thrust, and a popular field--health.

The popularity of the new health-related fields is reflected in the diversity of programs adopted in a variety of institutions. In Spring Arbor, Michigan, Spring Arbor College students can take a major in hospital administration. This major, which includes an internship in a local hospital, can be combined with courses in either business or the social sciences. Similarly, Oregon State University offers an interdisciplinary major in health care administration combining work in the Schools of Business, Health and Physical Education, and Home Economics. A medical technology major at Seattle University combines a liberal arts base with a year-long internship in a hospital.

As institutions design new programs of concentration, departments and colleges are sometimes combined in interesting departures from the status quo. At the University of Cincinnati, for example, there is an arrangement between the College of Arts and Sciences and the College of Business Administration by which the departments of English, German, and Romance languages offer two programs for students interested in business. A four-year program leads to a B.A. in English, German, French, or Spanish from the College of Arts and Sciences and a Certificate in General or International

Business from the College of Business
Administration. Students opting for this plan
major in one of the four languages and simultaneously follow a carefully selected schedule of
business courses. A five-year Co-op Program culmi-
nates in a B.A. in English, German, French, or
Spanish, a Certificate in General or International
Business, and a Certificate of Professional
Development. The course work of the five-year program is equivalent to that of the four-year plan.
Students are on campus for their freshman and sophomore years and alternate between work and study
quarters during the last three years.

To conclude this discussion of career-oriented
majors, it is illustrative to refer to one of the
comprehensive colleges and universities which led
the way in adopting such programs. Within the past
few years, Central Washington University has instituted new majors in health education, land studies,
law and justice, leisure services, mass media,
occupational safety and health, and vocational-
technical trade and industry. The Law and Justice
major merits special attention because it is a program within one of the most popular new areas of
concentration--law and criminal justice.

The Central Washington Program in Law and
Justice offers an interdisciplinary curriculum
designed to help train students for careers as
police officers, probation, parole, and corrections
workers, paralegal assistants, and court administrators. The program retains the humanistic emphasis
of the liberal arts degree while drawing from the
disciplines (primarily sociology, psychology, political science, and administration) those courses
which seem most suitable for persons wishing to
engage professionally in the law and justice system
or to prepare themselves for law school. The program attempts to provide courses which will enable
the student to appreciate the needs and underlying
theory of all segments of the law and justice
establishment in order that he may come to see himself and his professional activities in the larger
context suggested by this approach. To that end
both classroom and field experiences taught or
supervised by practicing professionals are offered.
Although more than half of the students registered
in the program are likely to enter the field of law
enforcement, liberal arts courses constitute the
bulk of the program. The program does not train
police officers but aims to provide the best in
higher education for police officers as well as

115

other students. Classes, both on and off campus, are tailored to suit the shifting tours of duty of many of the students, with the result that full-time and part-time, day, and evening students meet on common ground.

In summary, a clear majority of institutions seem to be moving in the direction of establishing new career-oriented majors. Though some defenders of the status quo see danger in any direct response by academe to the world of work, undergraduate concentration is becoming more closely linked to the marketplace by establishing new career-oriented majors, incorporating career-related minors into traditional major programs, and giving students the freedom to design their own career-oriented majors.

ISSUES IN PLANNING FOR CONCENTRATION

For several reasons, the notion of planning for concentration has been given scant attention at many institutions. On the one hand, some institutions have preferred to allow their majors to reflect the narrow needs of faculty as professionals and the requirements of graduate schools. On the other hand, many colleges and universities have responded to pressures for new majors with short-sighted adjustments. Often without thorough consideration, courses have been redesigned and new majors have been added while others have been deleted or allowed to lie dormant, while the relevance of liberal education for careers has fallen short of expectations. If institutions are to plan for concentration, three critical issues deserve special attention.

Issue 1: What Is the Role of the Major in
    Undergraduate Education?

In response to this question, Daniel Bell believes that most departments would reply: "to provide a basic minimum of specialization and coverage in a field." Considering this response inadequate, Bell asks to what end an individual acquires this specialization: "As a direct stepping-stone to graduate work in the field; to provide some knowledge of a particular discipline or subject as the background for professional or related work (e.g., in law or medicine); or what [Bell, 1966, p. 250]?" Bell found that at Columbia each department viewed its major mainly as a preparation for

116

graduate work in that subject.

Lewis Mayhew and Patrick Ford (1971) also believe that majors are designed to prepare students for graduate school and conclude that as a guide for structuring a major this purpose may be obsolete:

> There is a tendency to offer specialized courses at the upper division on the grounds that students need such specialization to prepare for graduate school or that a valid major must contain a high degree of specialization. We know, however, that the majority of undergraduate students do not enter careers related to their undergraduate majors, and that slightly less than half the students who attend graduate school do not concentrate on subjects in which they majored or concentrated as undergraduate students. And in view of the rapidly changing labor market, it seems likely that most who receive a bachelor's degree will shift their callings two, three, or four times during a lifetime. If the actual needs and desires of students for specialization were considered, offerings listed in college catalogs could be critically reduced, which might also solve the problem of the institution which offers more specialized courses than its faculty resources will allow [p. 154].

Asserting that concentration is meaningful only if it is done in an appropriate context, Mayhew and Ford recommend the requirement of a set of contextual courses. For example, courses in political science and economics would be contextual for a history major (Mayhew and Ford, 1971, p. 151). Perhaps the development of a context for a major is occurring even without formal requirements. The findings of the Carnegie Council study that students' electives tend to be selected from departments within the division of specialization, rather than from the major field itself, can be interpreted as student recognition of the need to place an area of specialization in a context (Blackburn, Armstrong, Conrad, Didham and McKune, 1976, p. 29).

Recent trends in graduate education support the expansion of areas of specialization. In an article on the plight of graduate schools, Malcom G. Scully notes the prevalent sentiment that "there should be less emphasis on research at the frontiers of knowledge and more emphasis on broad

117

understanding of the disciplines and the role it
plays in human culture [Chronicle of Higher
Education, April 24, 1978, p. 7]." Changes in the
structure of undergraduate majors may be stimulated
by modification of the purpose and design of graduate programs.

Preparation for graduate school has become, if
not the explicit purpose, at least the implicit
influencing factor for the major, in part due to
the organization of knowledge into disciplines and
the provenance of faculty from those specific disciplines. D. Richard Little believes that departments have emphasized preparation for graduate work
in the discipline because this is what they are
best staffed and trained to do (Little, 1974,
p. 100). A more critical observer contends that
majors have been dominated by "narrowed and selfish
departmental interests" (Thompson, 1976, p. 20).
Dwight Ladd found in his review of institutional
curriculum studies that very few colleges said much
about the form and content of the major. He concludes that the major "appears to be forbidden
territory for college or university committees, the
vigilantly guarded turf of the departments [Ladd,
1970, p. 181]."

Although majors at many institutions have been
designed on the assumption that graduate school is
the goal of each student, are there other goals
possible which might permit concentrations distinct
from the majors offered at the undergraduate level
in a specialized department of a graduate school?
A few writers have reflected on other possible roles
for the major. Charles Stanton (1976) believes
that faculty should adjust their approaches to
accommodate broader goals:

If arts and sciences faculty members would
envision their goals as two major functions--
the development of a milieu for exploration
and the training of specialized experts--they
would have great impact upon young people and
their personal development as well as the
training of scholars [p. 302].

William Sturner offers an analytic-action model
for liberal education in which the major programs
would be designed to unify the "steps of awareness,
interest, analysis and action" begun in the general
education program (Sturner, 1973, p. 155). He
believes that liberal education should not only be
the foundation but the guide for the specialized

118

modes of inquiry. Robert Hastings also indicates that concentrations should reflect and reinforce the goals of liberal education. He sets forth a value-action model challenging the disciplines to teach in such a way that students will seek to understand the impact of their actions and be able to make ethical and moral judgments (Hastings, 1974, p. 214).

While these suggestions indicate that a major has the potential for being more than graduate school preparation, the process of making it such requires more than simple curriculum adjustments. Nevertheless, interdisciplinary, student-designed, and career-oriented majors--in contrast to traditional discipline-based majors--do offer the possibility that undergraduate specialization can be more than preparation for graduate school.

Issue 2: What Is the Relationship of Concentration in Liberal Education to Career or Professional Preparation?

Perhaps the issue which has the most concrete impact on postsecondary institutions, especially those with a liberal arts emphasis, concerns the relationship of concentration to career or professional education. Curriculum planners have often emphasized that there is no conflict between liberal and professional objectives:

> . . . both the liberally educated and the professionally educated person must be rational and compassionate; he must be committed and tolerant; and he must be purposeful and flexible. He must be well versed in his basic disciplines, but also interested in his impact on people; he must be aware of and understand significant ideas and theories, but also committed to solving or alleviating the difficulties of individuals and society; he must understand and accept the necessity for rules and requirements in organizations and society, but also accept the need for flexibility in the application of these rules; he must sense and accept the existence of distinctions and differences, yet seek coherence, interrelationship, and comprehensive understanding. The truly liberally educated person is professional, and no one is truly professional who is not liberally educated [Dressel, 1971, p. 154].

119

Lindley Stiles calls liberal education the "tap root" for all professional training and performance. He believes that many of the dilemmas and controversies which professionals fail to confront adequately result from "too little liberal education, or perhaps from a failure of liberal education [Stiles, 1974, pp. 53-54]." Approaching the issue from a different perspective, Warren Thompson (1976) states:

> We should recognize that all undergraduate learning, properly understood and carried out, is "preprofessional" and "career oriented." It is a silly and dangerous charade to pretend otherwise. Since every student is preparing for something beyond his undergraduate years (call it "life" or the "real world" or whatever), why should we be reluctant to confess this [p. 21]?

From a theoretical point of view, there is no intrinsic incompatibility between traditional views of specialization in liberal education and career or professional education, although the historical emphasis on liberal education, to the exclusion of career education, has fostered the impression that some antipathy does exist. Therefore, as institutions consider new programs of concentration--especially career-oriented and student-designed majors--their efforts to wed those programs to their institutional conceptions of liberal undergraduate education should be deliberate and unremitting.

Issue 3: What Are the Criteria for Deciding Which Majors Are Appropriate in a Liberal Arts Setting?

Despite the potential compatibility of liberal and vocational education, one of the most persistent problems facing institutions today is the demand for additional majors with a high probability of employment upon receipt of the degree. If an institution is neither to stubbornly refuse to add or adapt majors nor to proliferate the number and type of majors it offers beyond the point of its ability to support them, on what basis can it make judicious decisions about which majors to add or adapt and which ones to reject or delete? Ultimately the criteria for such decisions will have to be established by each institution, but a few possible standards are mentioned in the literature.

John Heil offers two criteria: major programs should be aimed at the development of a theoretical understanding, and the implementation of majors should emphasize teaching (use of principles and theories) as opposed to training (learning to perform a specific activity) (Heil, 1974, pp. 312-313).

Earl McGrath (1974) mentions similar criteria:

> . . . if the integrity and the standards of a proper liberal arts college are to be preserved, the character and level of career preparation must be appropriate to an institution of higher education . . . . Instruction ought to be so grounded in theory as to achieve two objectives: (1) Even in a technical field it ought to provide the essential generalizations and principles to enable the student to apply what he learns to the wide variety of circumstances he will later encounter in his work, and (2) it ought so to prepare the student that he can preserve and enhance his competence as new knowledge and skills emerge and to inculcate the habit of doing so [pp. 288-289].

Both Heil and McGrath caution against adding new majors without consideration of their possible repercussions on other aspects of the curriculum and of the financial and personnel commitments necessary for their implementation.

Each of the three issues concerning the major requires a response by individual institutions, and it is probable that institutions will vary in the positions they take. What is essential is the process of articulating the issues, coming to acceptable institutional solutions, and then examining the content and structuring of the major in the light of those positions.

The external and internal pressures operating in higher education today have created an environment in which the undergraduate program has perhaps its greatest opportunity for impact on students by means of the area of specialization, not apart from it. The challenge to curriculum planners is to be aware of this opportunity and to adapt the structure, content, and purpose of the major so that the identified goals of undergraduate education can be achieved. With the resolution of the above issues, coupled with an awareness of the new arrangements for concentration, institutions are more likely to meet that challenge.

121

REFERENCES

Bell, Daniel. The Reforming of General Education. Garden City, New York: Doubleday, 1966.

Blackburn, Robert, Ellen Armstrong, Clifton Conrad, James Didham, and Thomas McKune. Changing Practices in Undergraduate Education. Berkeley, California: Carnegie Council on Policy Studies in Higher Education, 1976.

Carnegie Commission on Higher Education. A Classification of Institutions of Higher Education. Berkeley, California: Carnegie Commission of Higher Education, 1973.

The Carnegie Foundation for the Advancement of Teaching. Missions of the College Curriculum. San Francisco: Jossey-Bass, 1977.

College of Wooster. "Urban Quarter." Wooster, Ohio: College of Wooster, n.d.

Dressel, Paul L. College and University Curriculum. 2nd ed. Berkeley, California: McCutchan, 1971.

Dressel, Paul L. The Undergraduate Curriculum in Higher Education. New York: Center for Applied Research in Education, 1963.

Dressel, Paul L., and Frances H. DeLisle. Undergraduate Curriculum Trends. Washington, D.C.: American Council on Education, 1969.

Hastings, Robert F. "It's the Ripples that Sink Us." Liberal Education, 60 (1974): 209-214.

Heil, John. "Teaching, Training and the Liberal Arts Curriculum." Liberal Education, 60 (1974): 308-315.

Heiss, Ann. An Inventory of Academic Innovation and Reform. Berkeley, California: Carnegie Commission on Higher Education, 1973.

Howe, Florence. Seven Years Later: Women's Studies Programs in 1976. A Report of the National Advisory Council on Women's Educational Programs. Washington, D.C.: U.S. Government Printing Office, 1977.

Ladd, Dwight R. Change in Educational Policy. New York: McGraw-Hill, 1970.

Levine, Arthur, and John Weingart. Reform of Undergraduate Education. San Francisco: Jossey-Bass, 1973.

Little, D. Richard. "Beyond Careerism: The Revival of General Education." Journal of General Education, 26 (1974): 83-110.

Mayhew, Lewis B., and Patrick J. Ford. Changing the Curriculum. San Francisco: Jossey-Bass, 1971.

McGrath, Earl J. "Careers, Values and General
     Education." Liberal Education, 60 (1974):
     281-303.
Schmidt, George P. The Liberal Arts College. New
     Brunswick, New Jersey: Rutgers University
     Press, 1957.
Stanton, Charles J. "Reflections on
     'Vocationalized' Liberal Education."
     Educational Forum, 40 (1976): 297-302.
Stiles, Lindley J. "Liberal Education and the
     Professions." Journal of General Education,
     26 (1974): 53-64.
Sturner, William F. "An Analytic-Action Model for
     Liberal Education." Educational Record, 54
     (1973): 154-158.
Thompson, Warren. "Some Recurring Thoughts on
     Liberal Education." Liberal Education, 62
     (1976): 20-24.

5
Experiential Learning

It would be premature to say that experiential learning has finally come of age. Despite progress in some institutions and in some areas of professional and general education, it is still far from being a mature art or science. Understanding and practice are highly variable among institutions and programs across the country. For the most part experiential learning is still primitive. But interest in it is now strong and widespread and is not likely to diminish [Chickering, 1977, p. 12].

Experiential learning is one of the primary new forms of innovation in undergraduate education, and the purpose of this chapter is to examine the emerging types of experiential learning. The chapter begins with a definition of experiential learning, including a comparison with traditional learning, followed by a review of its historical antecedents. Five approaches to experiential learning form the skeletal framework for most of the chapter. These five categories are considered in detail, including examples and a discussion of the advantages and disadvantages of each form of experience. Finally, a discussion of several key issues in experiential learning closes out the chapter.

WHAT IS EXPERIENTIAL LEARNING?

On a first attempt to acquaint himself with experiential learning, the educator cannot help but be confused by the multitude of terms that accompany the concept. Field experience, prior learning, internship, cooperative education, service-learning, foreign study, intracultural experience, outdoor living, and individual enrichment are just some of the terms falling under the umbrella of experiential learning.

As a point of departure, the term may be segmented to distinguish between experiential learning occurring under the auspices of an academic institution and that which occurs prior to a student's matriculation. Robert Sexton and Richard Ungerer use two terms to make this distinction: "experiential learning" refers to prior experience while "experiential education" refers to experience concurrent with academic enrollment (Sexton and Ungerer, 1975, pp. 1-2.) According to this definition, experiential learning takes place entirely in a nonclassroom environment, occurs without specific educational objectives and without the supervision of academic staff, and is presented for credit after-the-fact. Experiential education, on the other hand, although also occurring outside the normal classroom experience, is carefully planned with specific educational objectives in mind, involves a mentor or faculty advisor to assist the student in learning, and is an integral part of current academic studies.

The treatment of experiential learning in this chapter encompasses both prior and current learning. It is defined as learning which possesses the following characteristics:

1. It occurs outside the normal classroom or laboratory environment.
2. Whether it occurs prior to or during academic enrollment, it is ultimately related to the student's educational objectives.
3. It is designed and evaluated with the assistance of a mentor or evaluator.
4. It may or may not be tied to career goals and the world of work.
5. It integrates learning with personal development.

A comparison of traditional and experiential learning may further clarify the concept. Traditional learning has several main characteristics:

1. It is limited to a classroom or laboratory setting.
2. It bases learning for the most part on abstractions and theory.
3. The faculty member serves as transmitter of knowledge, evaluator, and supervisor of

125

the learning.
4. A formal outline of readings and content organizes the process.
5. Learning is imparted in a standardized fashion for consumption by students who are assumed to be relatively homogeneous.

In contrast, experiential learning focuses on the variety and diversity available to learning:
1. It utilizes off-campus settings for learning (agencies, inner cities, industry, government, foreign countries, mountain ranges).
2. It focuses on the application of theories to solve real problems.
3. It depends heavily on the student's resourcefulness and ability to learn in an independent situation.
4. It recognizes the individuality of learning and the distinctiveness of each student's educational goals.
5. It recognizes the responsibility of colleges and universities to assure success to a variety of student populations.
6. It recognizes learning through doing accompanied by personal involvement and commitment.
7. It recognizes the student as an integral part of the planning and evaluation stages of learning.

According to David Kolb, experiential learning involves a four-stage cycle (Kolb in Chickering, 1977, pp. 17-18). First, the student becomes involved in a concrete experience. Second, on the basis of this experience, the student makes observations and reflections. Third, the student integrates concepts and generalizations into a theory to frame the experience and observations and to organize them for future use. Fourth, the student tests these observations in new situations and puts his theory into practice. This process is ongoing throughout the experience.

James Coleman describes experiential learning as almost the direct reverse of traditional learning, which he calls the "information assimilation process." Information assimilation occurs through receiving of information, organizing the information for the understanding of the general principle, inferring a particular application from the principle, and applying the principle. Experiential learning proceeds from the particular action and observations of its effects to understanding the

126

effects of that particular action, to deriving the general principle which encompasses that particular action, and finally to applying the generalization through action in a new circumstance. Coleman concludes that the steps in experiential learning are as legitimate as those in traditional classroom learning but are sequentially different (Coleman, 1976, pp. 50-58).

Experiential learning, then, is not an idle or chance happening which is granted credit. It is a learning process which demands involvement, contemplation, and action; it meshes the personal with the actual to create learning that is felt as well as abstracted. Indeed, at its best experiential learning encompasses skills, knowledge, application and personal growth. It recognizes the student as an individual who learns in unique ways and who has unique goals. Experiential learning tries to expand knowledge beyond the ivy-covered environment. Arthur Chickering emphasizes the challenge to experiential learning when he states that "the problem is to create that combination that is most effective for the person doing the learning and for the material to be learned [Chickering, 1977, p. 17]."

A BRIEF HISTORY OF EXPERIENTIAL LEARNING

John Dewey, in his book School and Society (1915), masterfully outlines for the field of education the relevance of experience to learning. He states:

> No number of object-lessons, got up as object-lessons for the sake of giving information, can afford even the shadow of a substitute for acquaintance with the plants and animals of the farm and garden acquired through actual living among them and caring for them. No training of sense-organs in school, introduced for the sake of training, can begin to compete with the alertness and fulness of sense-life that comes through daily intimacy and interest in familiar occupations. Verbal memory can be trained in committing tasks, a certain discipline of the reasoning powers can be acquired through lessons in science and mathematics; but, after all, this is somewhat remote and shadowy compared with the training of attention and of judgment that is acquired in having to do things with a real motive behind and

127

a real outcome ahead [pp. 11-12].

Although Dewey is one of the best-known proponents of experiential learning, the approach he advocates dates far back in the history of education. Socrates and Aristotle, for example, embraced a form of experiential learning--the dialogic method-- as the ideal process for arriving at the truth.

During the medieval period two types of guilds dominated learning and training. The one was a guild of scholars preparing for future experience; the other a guild of craftsmen whose apprentices learned through present experience. Interestingly, the craft guilds taught their apprentices some of the rudiments of general education (Olson, 1977, p. 8). Cyril Houle points out a third pattern of medieval learning which depended on experience: chivalry used practical application to teach young gentlemen the courtly arts and knighthood (Houle, 1976, p. 23). During the sixteenth and seventeenth centuries the practical-versus-theoretical debate focused on the role of mathematics and rhetoric (Olson, 1977, p. 11).

Frederick Rudolph notes that during the 1820s and 1830s in the United States, Ticknor, Abbott, Lindsey, Marsh, Jefferson, and others worked to meet more modern needs by including practical sub- jects in the classical curriculum (Rudolph, 1962, pp. 124-128). The impact of the Yale Report of 1828, however, reduced these early attempts to mere shadows of reform. It was not until the 1850s and 1860s that experiential learning assumed a greater importance in American higher education. The Morrill Act of 1862 opened the way for practical curricula in agriculture and the mechanical arts through the land-grant college, and its successor, the 1890 act, established practical subjects permanently in the curriculum. Johns Hopkins was the first medical school to use autopsy as a training tool in 1876, beginning an era of practical instructional techniques at medical schools, law schools, normal schools, and land-grant colleges (Houle, 1976, pp. 29-30).

In the twentieth century, cooperative programs were developed to integrate work experience and learning. In 1906 the University of Cincinnati permitted engineering students to alternate semes- ters of work and study, and Antioch College adopted the concept for liberal arts colleges in 1921 by expanding cooperative education to include all mem- bers of the student body (The Carnegie Foundation

for the Advancement of Teaching, 1977, p. 232).
Brooklyn College initiated the practice of granting
credits to adults for prior experience in 1954,
while three years later the University of Oklahoma
designed the first adult degree based on something
other than credits. The College-Level Examination
Program (CLEP) was started in 1965 and was introduced into practice in 1966. More recent developments include the establishment of groups whose
purpose is to expand the awareness and validation
procedures of experiential learning opportunities,
including the Society of Field Experience Education
(SFEE) in 1972 and the Cooperative Assessment of
Experiential Learning project (CAEL) in 1973.

Experiential learning has been an element of
education for centuries, chiefly through internships and practicums. Only recently, however, has
experiential learning become accepted as a legitimate form of learning in many colleges and universities. The following section discusses some of the
recent developments in education and the environment
which have created a favorable atmosphere for innovations in experiential learning.

NEW APPROACHES TO EXPERIENTIAL LEARNING

Surrounded by an environment which is consumer-
conscious, work- and life-integrating, and job-poor,
colleges and universities are confronted today by a
demand for accountability, made by many students
and parents who have invested in the system. The
traditional student population is shrinking both
because of a declining birth rate and because of
overall disenchantment with higher education.
Postsecondary institutions have been forced to consider new clienteles to serve.

Disadvantaged students are the primary new
clientele group to be attracted to higher education.
For several reasons, colleges and universities cannot always relate to these students as they have to
traditional students. First of all, traditional
classroom techniques are posited upon learning for
its own sake and delayed application. The new
learners often find such methods foreign to their
goals and needs. The disadvantaged student, who is
usually looking for mobility through the acquisition
of academic credentials, is without the traditional
background necessary for the task. Experiential
learning can be a source of motivation to such students by providing them with both immediate

involvement through the practical application of learning and self-assurance through a sense of accomplishment (Coleman, 1976, pp. 59-60).

A second new clientele is adult learners. The adult student brings prior experiences which are often valuable in relation to his educational objectives. The latter may tie into his employment and his need for certification in order to advance on the job. A strong desire exists among adult students for learning which has practical application. In addition, there is a desire that higher education recognize a student's prior accomplishments and help him relate those experiences to his certification. Arthur Chickering notes that many adults have learning goals that go beyond the concern for information and cognitive skills: developmental change is also an important goal (Chickering, 1976, p. 107).

In addition to serving new clienteles, the changing role of work in American society is a major impetus to experiential learning. An increasingly competitive job market has fostered a conscious evaluation by students of the practical skills and experiences derived from college. Students are demanding that education be more compatible with the reality of the nation's work needs. The student, as consumer, wants to know what he is getting from his education that will benefit him in his transition to the world of work.

Success in the workplace requires a certain amount of maturity in addition to technical skills. Sexton and Ungerer (1975) recognize the relevance of experiential learning to the developmental progress of the student when they state:

> Experiential education can be viewed as enhancing the maturation process of young people. Students participate in experiences where they learn how to accept responsibility and to be part of the adult society. Work settings afford the opportunities for youth to acquire vital maturation skills such as helping others who are less able and negotiating with others to protect one's rights, and to seek help when it is needed. Students are challenged to develop personal autonomy for their own learning and doing [p. 25].

Sheila Gordon concurs:

> . . . the college graduate entering the

130

workplace has multiple needs. He or she needs
to have a broad understanding of the dynamics
of the workplace and to be able to transfer to
those settings the general theories and
approaches learned in liberal arts and other
courses; to be able to sort out the distinctive
values, operating styles, and politics of the
workplace; to be prepared to understand his or
her own values and incentives within the context of that setting; to be able to measure
his or her own learning, growth, and performance in the experiential setting; and to be
able to recognize the need to modify or
upgrade technical skills learned in the classroom [p. 110].

Although many students do not seek professional
training at the undergraduate level, career exploration is frequently a major concern. The opportunity to explore the world of work and possible
careers is highly compatible with experiential
learning. Samuel Magill argues persuasively that
liberal education in the postmodern world should
include development of a sense of vocation (Magill,
1977, pp. 438-440).

These pressures for change have created new
dilemmas for higher education: How can it best
serve its new clienteles? Are its existing programs always compatible with the characteristics,
abilities, and needs of traditional as well as nontraditional students? What kind of programs can
best integrate experience and learning? In
response to these issues, a wide variety of experiential learning programs is being implemented at
colleges and universities. To do justice to the
variety of experiential programs, the following
sections focus on five distinct areas: work-learning
(cooperative education, internships, practica),
service-learning, cross-cultural experience
(foreign study, intracultural experience), academic
credit for prior learning, and individual growth
and development (outdoor living, individual enrichment).

Work-Learning Programs

Probably the most familiar of the five categories of experiential learning is work-learning.
It is useful to distinguish between three types of
work-learning programs. The first is the cooperative program in which the student alternates

classroom learning with work experience on a systematic basis throughout his college years. Second,
internships are practical work experiences which
are usually of a one-time nature and which frequently cap the senior year. Third, practica
expose the student to a work setting in an observer
role without significant responsibility.
Participation in these three types of work-learning
has increased dramatically in this decade. The
number of institutions involved rose from 125 in
1970 to over 1,000 in 1977; in 1977 the number of
participating employers reached 20,000 and the number of students was approximately 200,000 (Hyink,
1977, p. 4).

Although all three types of work-learning
experiences are widely used, the emphasis here will
be placed on cooperative programs, which are usually recognized as the purest form of work-learning.
Since the first program was begun at the University
of Cincinnati, the cooperative has become a popular
tool for combining classroom learning with practical
work experience. In addition to alternating terms
of work and study, the cooperative is usually characterized by:
1. Work of a professional nature directly
   related to the student's major or career
   objectives.
2. Inclusion in the curriculum as a credit
   course either within the major department
   or with a campus-wide course designation.
3. Evaluation of student performance by both
   the work supervisor and the faculty
   advisor.
4. Preferably full-time employment during the
   work semester.
5. Requirement for graduation in certain
   majors.
Cooperative programs are not necessarily related to the student's major field. In some colleges,
for example, the cooperative is designed to introduce the student to the general work world and to
act as a career exploration technique. The student
may participate for several semesters before determining upon a specific career objective and a
resulting major-related cooperative assignment.
Such exploration allows the student to test out
different professional options before investing
years of training in what might otherwise have been
an unsuitable career goal (Davis, 1972, p. 141).

Ideally, cooperative education offers the student a unique opportunity to integrate his learning

132

with the world of work as thought escapes the
abstraction of the classroom and work escapes the
limited realm of economics. Bernard Hyink (1977)
refers to this integrative process:

> Because of its very nature, cooperative educa-
> tion requires the student to demonstrate a
> mastery of various levels of thought.
> Frequently, students can perform well in their
> formal college and university courses, but
> they cannot apply what they have learned.
> Cooperative education affords this opportunity
> through job performance, to apply "classroom
> learning" to "real world" situations.
> Students are thus able to demonstrate the abil-
> ity to use ideas, principles, and theories in
> practical and concrete situations as encoun-
> tered at the co-op job site. Cooperative edu-
> cation also requires the students to extend
> the thought process beyond the level of appli-
> cation. The intellectual skills of analysis,
> synthesis, and evaluation are often required
> of students in the sciences as well as the
> liberal arts. The natural consequence of a
> theory well learned and successfully applied
> is the awarding of degree credit by the educa-
> tional institution [p. 13].

It is perhaps this capacity to involve several
levels of skills which has encouraged the United
States Civil Service Commission to create a plan by
which full-time cooperative students may enter
positions upon graduation through noncompetitive
and direct appointment. In his announcement of a
government-sponsored two-year internship program
for students completing graduate training in public
administration, President Carter recognized the
skills which can be gained in such programs:

> The concept is that [the students] would be
> bringing, along with a fresh approach and
> energy, several years of training or experience
> which would be directly relevant to federal
> problems . . . . I want to encourage younger
> people to consider a public service career. I
> also want to encourage the many university pro-
> grams which have committed important educa-
> tional resources to such training [SFEE &
> NCPSIP Newsletter, 1977, p. 4].

There must be recognized benefits for the

employer in the cooperative experience if the Civil
Service Commission is willing to create a direct
appointment privilege for cooperative students.
Such employer benefits include a proven talent pool
of permanent employees, a low turnover rate among
cooperative students hired after graduation in comparison with noncooperative graduates, more productive employees among cooperative graduates than
among recent graduates who had not previously
worked for the company, an influx of new ideas and
perspectives, and better channels of communication
between employers and the university (Hyink, 1977,
p. 27). A 1974 study at NASA's Langley Research
Center concluded that employers find the most positive results in career development when student
cooperatives are retained as permanent employees.
The study also found that cooperative students
advance more quickly (Jarrell in Sexton and Ungerer,
1975, p. 32). Another advantage to the employer is
the obvious manpower increase through the use of
student workers. Finally, the employer can play a
significant role in the training and development of
new professionals.

There are numerous potential advantages to the
student. Since the cooperative student is seen by
the employer as a potential recruit, the cooperative assignment as an avenue to future full-time
employment is the obvious student complement.
James Davis (1972) identifies several other benefits to students:
1. The individual financial benefits of coop-
    erative education are a major attraction,
    for students are able to anticipate
    scheduled employment periods. Spreading
    the demand for jobs throughout the school
    year and formalizing employer relations
    also enables students to make the most of
    a tight job market.
2. Students can continue their education
    through on-the-job training.
3. At its best, cooperative education can be
    liberal arts education for students.
    While some programs limit their objectives
    to providing students with the opportunity
    to earn money and hold employment in their
    fields of interest, others may expect stu-
    dents to learn to define and solve prob-
    lems, to recognize different value systems,
    to test theory against practice, and to
    appreciate knowledge both for its utility
    and for its own sake.

4. Students can learn the satisfactions and disadvantages of various careers before investing in years of costly education.
5. Finally, cooperative education programs can provide an exciting learning environment for the student developmental goal of identity discovery. Through these programs, students are able to grow in self-esteem and develop pride in accomplishment (pp. 140-142).

The institution also benefits from the cooperative program. Bernard Hyink notes that when offering credit for cooperative courses, the university counts participating students into its full-time equivalent figures--which is especially important to the public institution whose budget is driven by full-time equivalent students (Hyink, 1977, p. 12). Davis (1972) lists several benefits for the institutions participating in cooperative education:

1. Some institutions are able to achieve a distinctive identity through the adoption of cooperative education. The cultivation of a new image may, in turn, have positive implications for the recruitment of students and financial support.
2. Since year-round operation is necessary in many programs, facilities are better utilized and more students can be enrolled.
3. Through extending and building new relations with employers, institutions may improve their fund-raising ability and expand their general associations with the outside community (pp. 141-142).

In addition, the institution gains recognition for creating an atmosphere in which life, learning, and work are integrated.

There also are disadvantages frequently associated with cooperative programs. At first there may be student resistance to a cooperative program because additional time (usually a fifth year) may be needed to enable the student to complete his degree. Another problem is that although the student is earning while on the job, he may incur additional costs for transportation, clothing, and possibly food and housing depending on the location and type of assignment.

For the institution, problems of initial and continuing funding can be substantial. The expenses of setting up an office to initiate or coordinate cooperative programs are high and include travel, full-time professional and clerical staff salaries, and publications. Careful thought must be given to other cost and time elements such as faculty load, development of placements, matching of students with jobs, and supervision in the field. The institution must also make available to students any preemployment training that might be necessary (for example, a biology student with a laboratory placement might need to know dissection techniques or a student assigned to an industry library might need to know cataloging methods). The institution must provide a flexible academic calendar and class schedule in order to accommodate both its on- and off-campus students.

Inadequate and irregular enrollment also poses a problem. To maintain the optimal number of students on and off campus throughout the year is a challenge. Davis notes that the expense of establishing a cooperative education program is a minimal threat to institutional financial stability compared with the potential disaster which can result from mismanagement of enrollment flow in an established program (Davis, 1972, pp. 144-145).

A three-way network of responsibility among the student, the university, and the employer is developed by Joy Winkie (1971, pp. 133-144). The student needs to be cognizant of his responsibility for a fair day's work and for the reputation of the university. Students must also realize that though their pay may be low, the employer has a substantial training and monetary investment in them. The transition between education and the world of work needs to be supported by the employer and the university. Advising and counseling are important responsibilities of the supervisory personnel.

Finally, the university must realize that by granting credit for cooperative education it has committed itself to certain educational goals. Without such a commitment, participating faculty and students will suffer from dissonance between policy and attitude. Without faculty and administrative support in both dollars and credits, the experience of the cooperative student is relegated to second-class status.

Among the renowned cooperative programs are those at Northeastern University, Goddard College, and Antioch College. Cooperative education may vary in specifics from institution to institution, but the guiding principles remain essentially the same.

California State University, Fullerton,

136

established a University Center for Internships and Cooperative Education in 1973. The Center was designed to integrate the student's academic and professional work experiences. Partial funding for the Center during its first two years was provided by the California State University and Colleges Fund for Innovation, the university administration, and the Associated Students. Grant assistance from the U.S. Office of Education under Title IV, Cooperative Education, provided additional support from 1975 through 1977.

The University's location in Orange County, close to Los Angeles, creates a fertile area for potential work-learning assignments. Because the Center is responsible for coordinating practica, internships, and cooperative education, the development of contacts with employers is one of its central functions. A Campus Committee on Cooperative Education serves as an advisory body to the Center; the Committee includes faculty area coordinators, student representatives, representatives from the Placement Office, and the Director and Associate Director of the Center.

Each cooperative is a departmental or school course and is a salaried experience. Faculty area coordinators are assigned from each department or school to perform a variety of tasks including student counseling, assistance in setting up placements, on-site visits, and evaluation of student performance. Credit is given for the cooperative experience; the experience receives a letter grade in all cases except in the School of Business Administration and Economics and in the Theatre Department, where a credit/no credit determination is made.

To be recognized by the University as valid, work-learning experiences must meet three requirements: 1) the experience must be directly related to the student's major; 2) the experience must be included in the college curricula listings; and 3) the individual must meet minimum standards of work and performance as evaluated by the employer and faculty coordinator (Hyink, 1977, p. 2). In addition, the University strives to ensure that the cooperative is consonant with the student's ability and background.

Attempts are currently being made to expand the work-learning opportunities at Fullerton. The Center staff wants to increase the number of alternating term cooperatives, and hopes to increase career and life planning assistance to students. In

137

addition, the Center intends to continue to work closely with the community colleges in the California system on transfer of work-learning credits and continuance of student experiences when they leave the community college for the University.

Central Washington University in Ellensburg, Washington is another example of a college which is committed to the work-learning experience. Central Washington has an Office of Cooperative Education which coordinates the institution's Contracted Field Experience (CFE) and the Special Co-op Plan. The former involves internships of varied lengths; the latter is a two-year plan for students who wish to alternate terms of work and study.

The Special Co-op Plan is open to students at the Sophomore, Junior, and Senior levels. The student must remain in the program for eight consecutive terms. A student applies to enter the program one term prior to his desired initiation date, obtains approval from his faculty advisor, attends interviews with employers, and signs an agreement form. The general sequence for the co-op student is one pre-Co-op study term, six months field experience, two academic terms, six months field experience, and one post-Co-op study term. Internships must be closely related to the student's specific career interests and his academic major area of study. A student can still graduate in four years provided he attends two of the four summer terms while participating in the cooperative plan.

One of the better-known examples of cooperative education is the program at Antioch College in Yellow Springs, Ohio. Integration of work and study has been the primary force shaping the unique character of Antioch since the introduction of work-study in 1921.

Unlike the previous examples, Antioch requires the Experiential Education Program for all students in B.A. or B.S. programs. Students on four-year programs must complete six quarters of off-campus experience, and students on five-year programs must complete eight quarters. The Center for Experiential Education (CEE) helps place students in work assignments and assists them in designing their own assignments. (Antioch Education Abroad, travel, or special projects may be substituted for work.) Each student is assigned a faculty advisor from the Center upon his arrival on campus. The advisor assists the student in planning and evaluating all experiential learning.

Antioch does not require the student to be in

138

a work experience which is related to the major field. A student could work in construction, for example, and still fulfill the graduation requirement of experiential learning. The jobs are dependent on the skills which the students bring with them to college, especially in the case of freshmen. Occasionally, remuneration is no more than room and board or a small salary.

In addition to paid employment in city and country settings, off-campus experience may include creative projects or educationally valuable travel in the United States or abroad. Students can explore the demands and practical considerations of various careers through access to talents and resources not available in the classroom.

The opportunities offered through the Experiential Education Program are extensive, both in job content and geography. In recent years, for example, students have been employed by Visual Information Systems and Columbia Greenhouse Nursery in New York City; by the Biochemistry Department of Harvard University; by the Associated Press and the U.S. Treasury Department in Washington, D.C.; and by the Bay Area Rapid Transit and Mt. Zion Hospital in San Francisco. They have worked in camps, museums, city planning agencies, television stations, department stores, and libraries.

Antioch students have been operating room technicians and radio disc jockeys; newspaper copy boys and magazine writers; draftsmen and teachers; community organizers and government interns; research assistants and project supervisors. Each year Antioch students work for some 800 employers and in almost as many kinds of jobs.

To summarize, the amount of commitment within a student's department or college to work-learning can vary enormously both within and across institutions. Work-learning goals may be related to careers and majors or may be intended to improve the student's general ability to adjust to the work world. In some cases all students will be involved and in others only a small minority of students will participate. Moreover, the work-learning program may be short or stretched out over the entire college experience. Regardless of the form they take, work-learning programs are becoming an important feature of the undergraduate experience in many colleges and universities.

Service-Learning Programs

Large numbers of students with a commitment to public service are involved in service-learning programs. Robert Sigmon (1972) defines these programs as

> . . . the integration of the accomplishment of a task which meets human need with conscious educational growth. A service-learning internship is designed to provide students responsibility to meet a public need and a significant learning experience within a public or private institution for a specified period of time, usually 10 to 15 weeks [p. 2].

Samuel Magill couples the purpose of service-learning to a broader base when he describes liberal education as "a process of becoming uniquely human--to understand, to relate, to be purposeful about life, and to be committed to the task of shaping life for the good of the community [Magill, 1977, p. 442]." It is this concern for community which has encouraged students to participate in internships in agencies and institutions, usually with little, if any, remuneration. (This discussion will focus only on those service-learning experiences which grant credit. Noncredit service experiences are often initiated by the student without university involvement; although they may be valuable for student growth and skill-building, they do not relate specifically to educational objectives, nor does the university have a commitment to the experience.)

It is important to differentiate between service-learning and work-learning experiences. Although remuneration is the first difference to be noted, the pay differentiation is of less importance than other distinctions. More essential is the work-learning emphasis on personal objectives in terms of career goals and potential jobs, whereas service-learning emphasizes service to the public and the welfare of others. In the latter case, pursuit of career goals is secondary to serving the public good. As in the work-learning experience, the combination of action and reflection has implications for both education and vocation. However, the service-learning experience goes beyond techniques and the transition to the work world; it includes the development of a service lifestyle. William O'Connell contends that

service-learning suggests "the possibility of a
lifestyle of sensitivity, maturity, commitment, and
creativity [O'Connell, 1973, p. 5]."

Service-learning experiences are usually more
flexible than work-learning experiences, because
they can be as short as a weekend or as long as a
summer or semester. Although a student might participate in more than one experience, the alternating terms of work and study are not a characteristic
as in work-learning. Also, many service-learning
experiences are scheduled on a part-time basis while
students are taking classes. H. Merrill Goodwyn
(1973) lists eight objectives which are representative of most programs. They

1. Provide competent and highly motivated
   student manpower to public-service
   agencies.
2. Extend the process of higher education
   into the "real" world of public policy.
3. Give immediate manpower to agencies
   through student work.
4. Encourage youth to consider careers in
   public service.
5. Provide a pool of trained and qualified
   personnel for recruitment by the agencies.
6. Establish channels of communication
   between institutions and agencies.
7. Make resources of the university more
   accessible to the solution of community
   problems.
8. Provide constructive service opportunities
   for students seeking to participate in the
   solution of governmental and social problems (p. 36).

These goals suggest some of the benefits which
are commonly associated with the service-learning
concept. Robert Sexton and Richard Ungerer (1975)
delineate the benefits to the organization participating in the program as follows:

1. An immediate source of temporary manpower.
2. Screening and recruitment of future
   employees.
3. Access to skills and knowledge of academic
   institutions.
4. Opportunities for supervisors, as well as
   interns, to learn ways to manage work and
   learning for themselves.
5. Opportunities to examine the learning and
   teaching dimensions of their own organizations.

141

6. Access to thoughts and attitudes of the young (ventilation).
7. Invigoration of permanent staff through the presence of students.
8. Fostering creditable witnesses (interns and faculty) about the nature and worth of the organizations in promoting the public interest [p. 34].

Benefits also exist for students, including the opportunity to experience personal development and growth, to apply academic knowledge to practical tasks, and to provide direct public service. In summarizing the results of a study of service-learning programs at Mars Hill College, O'Connell states that interns gained

. . . an increase in understanding community problems, public needs, and the realities that affect solutions to these problems and needs, . . . learned a great deal about people very different from themselves and ways they might or might not work with these fellow members of society . . . [and] gained new skills in identifying specific, practical problems and independently determining ways to deal with them [O'Connell, 1973, p. 7].

David Kiel expresses the benefits to the student in such programs in the following terms:

1. Students develop more helpful, knowledgeable, and concerned attitudes toward community problem-solving.
2. Students experience an increased motivation to work and learn in public need settings after learning to work effectively with others in internships.
3. Students learn a great deal about their personal abilities and cultural commitments.
4. There is an immediate impact on the students' behavior and on their plans for the future [Kiel in Sigmon, 1974, p. 26].

Finally, Harlan Cooper (1974) refers to the internship from the student perspective:

You are able to become involved in significant issues and problems, and at the same time, maintain your independence. And most significantly, you have the opportunity to make a

142

difference. Whichever agency you serve with, your actions have consequences that affect the way other people live [Cooper in Sexton and Ungerer, 1975, p. 35].

Although service-learning internships are in general regarded as successful, there are certain potential disadvantages to the programs. Sexton and Ungerer draw attention to the problem that in programs which exist solely because of student man-power, student learning can become secondary to the service (Sexton and Ungerer, 1975, p. 35). The agency and institution need to carefully balance the service and learning components so that one does not suffer through the other's dominance. Donald Eberly (1974) suggests a possible solution to the balance question:

The best assurance of balance seems to come about when the employer/supervisor has a vested interest in getting a good performance out of the student, and teacher/professor has a vested interest in extending the intellect of the student and of assessing that extension [p. 2].

Raymond Shapek reiterates the two-fold nature of the experience in his contention

. . . that it provide a needed service to the sponsoring agency and that it is a learning experience for the participants, particularly the intern. Service-learning is the integra-tion of the accomplishment of a needed task with educational growth [Shapek in Sexton and Ungerer, 1975, p. 36].

Suzanne Buckle and Leonard Buckle identify eth-ical concerns in the three areas of protection of the community, the relationship between the univer-sity and the professional agency, and undue respon-sibility for the students who are involved in poli-tically active situations (Buckle and Buckle in Sexton and Ungerer, 1975, p. 36). Also, institu-tions must be cognizant of the costs involved for students who are not paid (or paid little) and who may incur expenses beyond the usual college costs unless they are working in home or college communities. In addition, the problems of transition from education to work must be recognized; some students may not adjust well and may therefore fail or be assigned to menial tasks as a result. Finally, the

143

effective service-learning program requires heavy institutional support and commitment. A deep belief in the credit value of service-learning and in the purpose behind it is essential if the experience is to gain credibility with students, faculty, and outside agencies.

One of the early participants in developing the comprehensive service-learning internship concept was the Southern Regional Education Board (SREB), which began its efforts in the late 1960s. SREB began to develop internships within its own region and later turned its efforts toward the decentralization of the program throughout the states once the concept took hold.

The University of Kentucky in Lexington is an excellent example of a large state university which has become increasingly involved in the idea of service-learning as one type of experiential learning program. Each semester approximately 2,500 students are engaged in some type of preplanned off-campus educational activity for academic credit. The Office for Experiential Education (OEE), under the Dean of Undergraduate Studies, assists interested students in developing a semester of experiential learning for academic credit. Students may choose to take advantage of the many field placements coordinated by the OEE or to create an individual program. OEE staff counsel students about the opportunities available and provide referrals to appropriate academic departments for credit arrangements.

The possibilities for field learning are limited only by student creativity and interest. A classics major might work with a museum, a history major might collect the oral records of an area, and a psychology major might assist with the research of a mental health agency. However, there are several specific programs available: the University Year for Action Program, the Frankfort Administrative and Legislative Intern Programs, and the Lexington-Fayette Metro Government Internship Program.

By way of example, the Frankfort Administrative and Legislative Intern Programs have been developed by the state government to encourage Kentucky's college students to become directly involved in governmental activity. In the Administrative Intern Program, students spend seven months in professional positions in state government for which they receive full academic credit and a salary. Assignments vary by semester but have included major cabinets such as Development, Transportation, Consumer Protection, Justice, and Environmental Protection, as well as such agencies as Personnel, Public Information, and Finance. Legislative interns spend one semester in Frankfort during the General Assembly and work directly with legislative committees and members of the General Assembly.

The OEE has developed one internship program which is designed to explore the ethical dimensions of public policy decision making.

> The program is an attempt at combining intern-
> ships and an interdisciplinary seminar in
> order to teach a liberal arts concept (ethics)
> in a manner that would lead to a deeper under-
> standing and internalization than if taught
> solely in the classroom. Fifteen students
> each semester, from different disciplines, are
> placed in public service internships in which
> they are able to examine and participate in
> professional decision making and in a seminar
> in which they reflect upon the ethical nature
> of these decisions and create a theoretical
> framework for how these decisions ought to be
> made [Hofer, Sexton, and Yanarella, 1976,
> p. 171].

The internships are with local and state govern-
ments and advocacy organizations. Examples of such
placements include the City-County Planning
Commission, a legal services group, the State
Commission on Women, a farmers' cooperative, the
Human Rights Commission, and the State Legislature.
Most students receive credit for a full semester for
the experience by combining three seminar credits
with other contract experiential learning courses
arranged through faculty in their major departments.
In a recent session of the course, students kept
journals, read assigned literature, participated in
a trip to Washington, D.C., wrote an individual
final paper, and met with one of the faculty team
members to discuss their journals (Hofer, Sexton,
and Yanarella, 1976, pp. 182-183).

Cross-Cultural Experiences

A third category of experiential learning consists of cross-cultural experiences. As employed
here, this category includes the subcategories of
foreign study programs and intracultural programs.
The former are well-known for the opportunities

they offer students to observe and study in a culture different from their homeland. Intracultural programs encourage the student to explore a subculture within his own country.

Foreign Study Programs. Foreign study programs find their antecedents far back in history. In 301 B.C., for example, Zeno the Stoic founded a school in Athens to bring Greeks and foreigners together to promote world community (Student Advisory Committee, CIEE, 1973, p. i). More recently, the concept of the Grand Tour was popular from the sixteenth through the eighteenth centuries, although according to Kenneth Charlton, the purpose of the Grand Tour had changed by the eighteenth century:

> Whereas the chief purpose of the Grand Tour in the eighteenth century was cultural, this was not the case in its nascent years in the sixteenth and seventeenth centuries. Then the aim was strictly "useful" and "practical": to gain practical experience of other countries, of foreign people, of their languages, and of the terrain and resources of these countries, all of which would be useful in a future diplomatic or political career [Olson, 1977, p. 13].

The pursuit of graduate study was an important influence on travel abroad during the nineteenth century. Many Americans made the trip to England, France, or Germany to pursue advanced learning in disciplines not offered in the United States. Today such travels may satisfy several desires at once: culture, practical language experience, exposure to other peoples, and possibly career goals (e.g., foreign service, translating).
During the 1920s, foreign study received an additional impetus through the extension of the League of Nations philosophy. The Rhodes Scholars program was one of the initial formalized efforts. The full impact of the approach did not come until the 1950s, following the rebuilding of Europe. The improvement of communications and the ease of travel increasingly spurred growth. The Fulbright Program was one of the first in the postwar era of foreign study.
While the main emphasis here will be on foreign study, a brief glimpse of parallel experiences gained through foreign work and travel is

appropriate. A number of students each year work abroad in either part-time or full-time jobs. The work experience is rarely given credit by universities for several reasons. Most important, the work available to students living abroad is almost never above the menial level of resort work, restaurant jobs, or au pair positions. The number of placements of a professional nature is negligible. Work abroad is very difficult to obtain both because of the long-distance search and because many countries have stringent work laws as a result of high unemployment and a desire to save preferred positions for their own citizens. Although ideally a work experience might provide a greater opportunity than classwork to see the "real" country and to take advantage of its cultural experiences, since the rigors of academics are not involved, it is difficult to evaluate any student learning that might occur. Many students also take advantage of opportunities to see other cultures through informal travel. Again, because they are unable to demonstrate the relevance of travel to specific educational goals, few students are able to obtain credit for such experiences.

Foreign study usually takes one of several organizational forms. It may involve study through a program initiated by a foreign university for American students, study provided through an ongoing agreement between the home university and a foreign institution, reciprocal exchange programs between the home university and the foreign institution, study in a foreign university sponsored by a consortium of colleges, study at a transplant American campus, or individually-designed programs. Each of these arrangements makes certain assumptions about foreign study.

The foreign university's program for American students creates a setting in which Americans can study together either in English or in special classes conducted at a suitable level of the foreign language. Although language difficulties can thus be eliminated or diminished, this type of program often results in an artificial surrounding which can become too "Americanized" for an accurate view of the foreign culture. In contrast, the ongoing exchange between the home university and the foreign institution recognizes a university commitment to a well-planned and evaluated foreign study program. Likewise, a reciprocity agreement between two universities encourages contacts, recognizes the worth of foreign study to both cultures,

147

and encourages full commitment on both sides.

The consortium approach to foreign study has several advantages. Individual colleges, although interested in and educationally committed to foreign programs, may not have the resources to launch a program or the variety of programs they would like. Few colleges would be able to support actively programs of their own in more than one or two countries. By establishing a consortium, colleges pool financial and time resources, expand the offerings to include additional countries, and help to ensure full enrollment in each program.

The transplanted American campus originally made good financial sense for the American college; education abroad had sound merit, and no college could scoff at the savings gained by educating students abroad rather than at home. At current exchange rates, however, the monetary advantages of this approach have disappeared. Further, the transplanted American campus, like the foreign program for Americans, is often accused of artificiality. An advantage, though, is the presence of university staff who integrate the experiences, ensure the university's commitment, and protect the university's academic standards.

Individually-designed programs are in a minority. Few students have the sense of adventure to undertake an experience which has not had the benefit of being tested by preceding students. In addition, this type of experience requires extensive prior research and time to design so that all facets are considered. It is probably unfortunate that this option is rarely utilized, since such programs are highly compatible with experiential learning in that they are tailored specifically to the individual student's educational objectives and personal growth.

The wide variety of program options suggests the popularity of foreign studies. In 1950 only six programs offered credit to undergraduates for foreign study during the academic year (Brick and McGrath, 1969, p. 41). By 1978 there were 763 academic-year programs and 826 summer programs sponsored by American universities (Cohen, 1978). Foreign study is available in nearly every Western European country, Africa, South America, the Near East, and the Far East.

A number of other service and living options are also available. The Experiment in International Living sends more than 2,000 students to forty nations each year to live with families. Many

religious organizations and civic clubs also spon-
sor family experiences and work camps. UNESCO
sponsors a Coordination Committee for International
Voluntary Workshops. Job placement is facilitated
by several agencies, including the International
Association of Students in Economics and Business
(AIESEC), the International Association for the
Exchange of Students for Technical Experience, and
a branch of the American Institute for Foreign
Study (EUROJOB). The Council on International
Educational Exchange (CIEE) is also very active in
assisting students and colleges interested in for-
eign experiences.

The advantages of experiential learning involv-
ing foreign study are fairly obvious. The broadening of one's perspective to include another culture
and the resulting self-examination are well-
accepted. The acquisition of further language
skills and the investigation of fine arts and literature in their natural setting are established as
valid learning experiences.

Less publicized are the disadvantages of foreign study programs. A critical issue for the participating institution is the quality of the program
offered by the foreign university and the implications this has for the respectability of the credit
granted. The more stringent the academic standards
of the home university, the more acute this problem
may become. The foreign university must be carefully evaluated before credit is accepted for the
experience. In fact, unless an ongoing relationship between the university and the foreign institution ensures updated information, the evaluation
might be obsolete within a few years. The proliferation of available programs and the rapid changes
within them can quickly outdate even a carefully
detailed evaluation.

Closely tied to the quality issue for the university is how the latter views the involvement in
foreign study in terms of its educational mission.
A firm commitment to the value of the experiences
and the offering of credit is essential if the foreign study option is to gain legitimacy and be
utilized by students. Without such a commitment,
administrative problems may cause the learning
experiences to be abandoned as too time-consuming
or may create a negative attitude toward such programs.

The issue of credit is probably the most
crucial to the student involved in the experience.
At many colleges the credit value of the experience

will not be determined until after the student
returns or, at the earliest, during his time abroad.
Long-distance communication difficulties often mean
that insufficient materials are available prior to
the departure of the student, forcing the postpone-
ment of evaluation. As a result, the student may
find upon his return that his year, however valuable
to him, will receive no credit from the home university. Many students are discouraged from taking
the experience at such risks. A university should
provide detailed guidelines for earning credit to
ensure that the process is as clear and fair as
possible. Academic advising prior to the student's
decision to participate should be accurate and
realistic.

Of course, the student needs to give careful
consideration to how foreign study fits his educational goals. Unless the participant is able to
determine the specific objectives to be fulfilled
by such programs, he is unlikely to gain the maximum benefit from the program, is unable to tailor
the experience to his needs, and is likely to be
totally dissuaded because of credit risks.

Other potential disadvantages include:

1. Many universities require the participating student to withdraw from the college.
   For some students (and for more parents),
   this withdrawal attaches a stigma to the
   experience. Even if a student feels that
   the withdrawal policy itself is reasonable,
   when coupled with the second disadvantage
   it can be demoralizing.

2. Because many programs are not university-
   sponsored, some colleges feel no responsibility to or interest in the student while
   he is abroad. At colleges where there is
   a full-time foreign study office, this
   insensitivity is somewhat lessened by
   assistance with the details of the semester after the student's return (such as
   housing and preregistration).

3. Just as classroom experience at home can
   leave little time to absorb the cultural
   and intellectual atmosphere outside the
   classroom, the academic experience abroad
   can also be unexpectedly limiting.

4. High financial commitment is required from
   the student. Even in university-sponsored
   programs which include tuition, airfare,
   and housing in the package fee, costs for
   independent travel, food, and incidentals

are usually the responsibility of the student.

The university must acknowledge that if it wishes to actively encourage foreign study among its students, it must be willing to provide adequate financing, extensive advisement, and equitable credit procedures. When separate departments handle different programs, information may be scattered and coordination lacking. The use of a volunteer office to oversee foreign study, although a start, is often inadequate because of lack of continuity, scarcity of funds, and limited staff hours. The assignment of a permanent position and adequate staff support, as well as money for the purchase of library materials and supplies, is usually necessary. Despite these concerns, foreign study programs are growing rapidly in number. Colleges and universities are seeking better ways to assist students who want to take advantage of such opportunities.

Intracultural Programs. The intracultural experience is similar to the foreign study experience in several ways. Like the foreign study option, the subculture alternative promotes the understanding of a different cultural milieu. Participants are encouraged to observe and analyze an alternative culture and, in turn, reexamine their own subculture--just as in the foreign study experience. While foreign study emphasizes international differences and similarities, the intracultural experience emphasizes the differences within the student's own culture.

There are other important distinctions between the two types of experiences. First, the intracultural experience usually calls for a participant-observer role while the foreign experience is more likely to require a student role. The intracultural experience is probably not a classroom experience, but is rather one of living and working within a different community to find out as much as possible about the subculture. Second, where the exchange unit of foreign study is normally classroom credits, the intracultural experience depends on journals, final papers, and seminar discussions for its value.

The intracultural experience stresses the experience itself and the growth obtained through it. The foreign study alternative stresses courses taken and considers the out-of-classroom experience to be secondary to credit. John Duley argues that the intracultural option is usually tied to liberal skills such as the development of information

151

sources, cultural understanding, interpersonal communication, commitment to relationships, decision making, self-reliance, self-understanding, and written communication (Duley, 1974, pp. 14-15). In contrast, the foreign study option focuses on language skills or knowledge acquired through the academic disciplines; although the variety of experiences is greater in the foreign study option, the cultural baggage brought home by the student is seldom tied to other liberal arts goals.

The advantages of intracultural learning are several. The student as a participant-observer becomes immersed in an experience which encourages not only cultural awareness but also personal growth through interrelationships and self-examination. Such experiences not only develop observation skills but also foster the skills of written and verbal communication through seminar discussions and report-writing. In pre- and post-seminars students compare experiences, share feelings, and seek peer and faculty comment through more than casual conversations.

The most apparent disadvantages of this type of program are the staffing and financial commitments involved. Faculty advising and seminar staffing are critical to the learning process. Careful placement choices are needed to ensure both learning and safety for the student. Because students need certain skills before entering the experience (for example, critical incident writing), the pre-seminar is as important a staffing commitment as the postseminar. Evaluation is difficult due to the frequently unsupervised nature of the actual experience and because of the personal growth elements. If the learning site is located some distance from the college, students may also incur substantial traveling costs in attending academic seminars during the experience.

Foreign study and intracultural options are both attractive alternatives to traditional learning. To illuminate the large selection of foreign study programs and increase the familiarity of most readers with this option, several examples of cross-cultural experiences are examined below.

Goshen College in Goshen, Indiana is unique in its approach to foreign study. In 1968, Goshen instituted the Study Service Trimester (SST) for all students as part of the general education requirements. Goshen's four objectives for the program are: 1) to examine and experience another culture; 2) to gain the experience of serving in a

practical way; 3) to experience an intensive relationship with a group of Goshen students and faculty; and 4) to contribute to a climate of international interest and understanding on campus.

Goshen students may participate in SST any
time after the second trimester of their Freshman
year, with the majority of students choosing to go
during their Sophomore year. To participate, the
student need only preregister two trimesters in
advance and be screened by the SST Office. The fee
charged includes the student's transportation, room
and board, and tuition for the fourteen weeks. Host
countries usually include Costa Rica, Nicaragua,
Honduras, Guadeloupe, Jamaica, Haiti, Belize, and
El Salvador. Slightly higher fees may be charged
if students attend special programs in Korea,
Poland or Germany.

Goshen purposely chose to place the SST experience in developing countries for several reasons:
the student must break completely from his own culture; the student is exposed to human need and can
work at understanding this reality; the student
lives in another culture so as to be exposed to
every facet of it; and the student has a chance to
see Christian servanthood at work in a needy society. Just as purposeful are the College's attempts
to acquaint students with the host country's customs and language before sending them into the rural
areas to serve the nationals in some capacity,
rather than to merely attend classes in a foreign
university.

The students travel in a group of approximately
nineteen persons. A Goshen faculty member on leave
(accompanied by his family if he is married)
directs the program in the host country. During
the first seven weeks of the trimester, the language and customs are emphasized; the second seven
weeks are devoted to the field experience.
Throughout the experience the students live in the
homes of nationals and eat two meals a day with
their host families. A number of learning techniques are used during the first segment of SST,
including field trips, discussions with local offi-
cials, lectures by artists, and journal keeping.
The second segment may find a student assisting in
day care centers, government hospitals, recreation
programs, or midwife/child care/nutrition programs,
or teaching in local schools.

The twelve trimester hours granted for SST
include credits for social science (4), humanities
(3), natural sciences (1), and foreign language (4).

153

In English-speaking countries, students take a four-hour independent study instead of language work. More hours can be given for foreign language if tests indicate that student proficiency warrants them. The courses are evaluated on a credit/noncredit basis, except for the foreign language and independent study hours which may be taken for either a letter grade or credit/noncredit.

Of the Goshen students, 85 percent participate in the SST experience. Students who select an on-campus option to SST must take a minimum of fourteen hours in area studies, international concerns, or anthropology. A student who has lived in a country outside of North America for at least six months after high school or two years after the age of twelve or who has participated in a church or service-sponsored agency in a different cultural setting can receive partial credit toward the on-campus option. International students do not have to elect the SST.

Although more conventional in its foreign study options than Goshen, Aquinas College in Grand Rapids, Michigan also adds a twist to its program which makes it different from the more typical foreign study experience. Students at Aquinas may enroll in a semester-long Ireland Overseas Study Program. The College uses thatched cottages in the Connemara region of County Galway in Western Ireland as its campus. Approximately thirty students and two instructors are involved in the semester experience, which is offered once a year. Although guest spaces are sometimes available, the College primarily selects its own students who have at least sophomore status and who are full-time. Students receive a minimum of twelve and a maximum of twenty semester hours for the program.

The curriculum centers around several aspects of Irish Studies. All students enroll in two core courses. In a recent term, Irish Literary Heritage and Physical Geography of Ireland were the required courses. In addition to these two core courses of four semester hours each, students can choose from a wide range of Irish Studies modules in the humanities, social sciences, and natural sciences. Weekends are usually kept open for student travel. A ten-day period midway through the semester is also available for student travel, and students are required to vacate the residences during this time.

Justin Morrill College of Michigan State University combines both intracultural study and foreign study in its cross-cultural option.

Students enrolled in Justin Morrill College must participate in a one-term off-campus field experience to meet graduation requirements. In the cross-cultural option for this field experience a student may elect to become involved in either a foreign culture or a subculture of his own country for a minimum of nine weeks. Approximately 60 percent of the students choose a foreign study experience and the remaining 40 percent opt for an intracultural experience. Students desiring cross-cultural experiences must arrange their own placements, must plan opportunities for active involvement in a new culture, and must have arrangements nearly finalized before enrolling for credit (Duley, 1974, p. 14).

Students enroll in a five- to six-week seminar in the semester prior to their field experience. The seminar meets several hours each week, including the first Saturday after the seminar begins. This Saturday meeting is designed to expose the student to the strangeness of being immersed in a new culture. The students are informed only that they will be dropped in a small Michigan community in the morning where they spend the day trying to learn as much as possible about the new environment. This experience requires the student to decide what is important to learn and to develop a strategy to gain that information. An afternoon debriefing enables students to share significant happenings. Follow-up conferences with faculty explore the critical incidents further and the student's feelings about the experience. This preparation seminar has as its objectives to increase students' skills in observation, to train students in critical incident writing, to initiate journals, to introduce students to disorienting experiences, to introduce self-initiated learning contracts, and to give experience in values clarification (Duley, 1974, pp. 16-18).

John Flanagan's Critical Incident Technique (C.I.T.) has been adapted to the program and students are required to use this technique in writing up nine incidents during their field experience. The objectives of the latter include developing skills in finding information sources, cultural understanding, interpersonal communication, commitment to persons and relationships during the experience, decision-making skills, self-understanding, self-reliance, and written communication skills (Duley, 1974, pp. 14-16).

A follow-up seminar is held after the student returns from the field experience. In preparation the student holds a conference with a faculty

155

member to select one of his nine critical incidents for seminar presentation. During the five- to six-week seminar the students present their critical incidents and are then interviewed by other members of the seminar. A pass/no credit evaluation is made for the total experience.

These examples show that foreign study and intracultural experiences can take on unique aspects from one college to the next. Goshen expands the concept of foreign study to include service to others, exposure to developing countries, shared learning experience, and a general education requirement for graduation. Aquinas College also opts for the group approach, but chooses a rural campus and offers more traditional coursework as well as travel opportunities. Justin Morrill emphasizes the individual experience, observation skills, pre- and post-seminars, and looks both outward to other cultures and inward to subcultures here at home.

Academic Credit for Prior Learning

Prior learning, that learning which has taken place before enrollment in a college or university, has several characteristics that distinguish it from what occurs in an institutional setting. No specific educational objectives were outlined before the prior learning experience; the experience lacks the supervision of academic staff; it potentially combines work, life, and community service; it occurs entirely outside the academic milieu; credit for student experience is given after the fact; its evaluation and certification functions are relegated entirely to postsecondary institutions.

The inclusion of prior learning as a legitimate form of experiential education is still under consideration in many institutions. Fine distinctions between experiential education and experiential learning or between sponsored and prior learning might permit prior learning to be excluded from experiential learning. Nevertheless, there has been increased receptivity to the idea of awarding credit for prior learning in the last several years. Arthur Chickering, although he separates sponsored and prior learning, raises the question, "If we add to our courses learning demonstrated by performance in experiential settings--on a job, in a volunteer activity, through a field project--then can we ignore such evidence when a new student comes to us and asks that it be credited [Chickering, 1977,

p. 42]?"

Morris Keeton identifies four factors in the last decade which create a receptive atmosphere for prior learning: education has recognized that it has made too sharp of a distinction between life and learning; the community college has expanded the range of subjects to include the affective domain; colleges are more serious now about recruiting and serving adults; and national commissions and other external forces have supported increased flexibility (Keeton 1976, p. xi).

In Academic Credit for Prior Off-Campus Learning (1975), David Trivett provides a summary of surveys on prior learning. He concludes that because of the nongeneralizable results of most questionnaires and the somewhat biased rates of return, it is difficult to establish the actual number of institutions that are granting credit for prior learning. However, data can be summarized to the extent that college and university interest in prior learning is on the increase and that credit by exam for prior learning is more prevalent than credit based on work or life experiences (Trivett, 1975, pp. 10-13).

There are three major procedures for granting credit for prior learning: credit by examination, credit for training or learning through a noncollegiate organization, and credit for prior life and work experiences. Examination for college level credit is the most popular method, and the College Level Examination Program (CLEP) is the most widely-used testing procedure. Others include the American College Testing Service (ACT) examinations, the New York Regents' College Proficiency Examination Program (CPEP), and examinations offered by individual institutions. The second procedure encompasses sources such as the Office of Educational Credit (OEC), the Defense Activity for Non-Traditional Education Support (DANTES), and other noncollegiate organizations. Credit for prior life and work experience varies greatly from institution to institution. (External degree programs, which are discussed in the next chapter, often grant credit by all three methods.)

As noted above, CLEP is the most widely-used examination program for validating prior learning. A purpose of CLEP is

. . . to enable those who have reached the college level of education outside the classroom--through correspondence study, television

courses, on-the-job training, or other means,
traditional or nontraditional--to demonstrate
their achievement and to use the test results
in seeking college credit or placement
[Educational Testing Service, 1970, pp. 19-
20].

The format of CLEP includes both general examinations for basic liberal arts areas and subject
examinations designed to measure achievement in
specific disciplines. It is important to note that
CLEP scores do not in and of themselves equal
credit. Instead, a measurement of knowledge is
forwarded to institutions for internal use in evaluating prior learning and granting credits.
    A second purpose of the CLEP test should be
noted in order to appreciate David Trivett's contention that CLEP may be reaching traditional students better than nontraditional students (Trivett,
1975, pp. 32-33).

    The Program may also help students already
    enrolled in college who wish to transfer from
    one collegiate institution to another. In
    addition, some colleges encourage independent
    study and recognize the examinations as an
    alternate route for meeting course require-
    ments [Educational Testing Service, 1970,
    p. 20].

The traditional student usually becomes aware of
CLEP through faculty advisors, counseling centers,
and so on. The nontraditional student is less
likely to be aware of CLEP, despite efforts to
advertise in magazines and to notify people about
the examination through public libraries.
    Every college and university should have a
stated policy concerning credit for CLEP.
Furthermore, all concerned in the college community
should know exactly what procedures are in effect
and what limitations are placed on CLEP at that
institution. Specifics about cut-off scores, eli-
gibility to take the exams, the right of a professor
to disallow test credit for his field, and whether
examinations must be tied to specific courses must
also be addressed (Trivett, 1975, p. 26). As with
any standardized test, proper usage depends on
understanding the meaning of the norms. Despite
these cautions concerning CLEP examinations, the
number of students who participate in this and
other testing programs is significant.

The second common method for recommendation of
college credit is through OEC or DANTES. The
Office of Educational Credit is the successor to
the American Council on Education's Commission on
Accreditation of Service Experience (CASE). Unlike
CASE, the OEC evaluates and recommends credit not
only for military experience but also for learning
acquired through noneducational organizations
(Trivett, 1975, p. 34). The OEC publishes the
Guide for educators who wish to consider granting
credit for military courses. The Guide recommends
credit on four levels and with specific credit
hours. The advantages of this program are that it
is under continual review, and, being voluntary,
does not represent a threat to institutional
autonomy (Trivett, 1975, p. 38).

The third method of obtaining academic credit
is through the evaluation of the actual experiences
of the student. The portfolio is a common method
of evaluating prior learning from life and work
experiences. Usually the portfolio will include a
vita, a narrative of the student's background and
educational goals, a request for credit, and documentation (certificates, letters, samples of work).
The portfolio should reflect careful analysis and
organization of the experiences. For obvious
reasons, counseling is an important support service
to portfolio development. The student is normally
responsible for the identification of the experiences to be evaluated, for the explanation of the
learning, and for sufficient documentation; the
college is responsible for measurement, evaluation,
and transcript generation.

There are many attitudinal barriers to the
acceptance of prior learning. Resistance to change,
faculty who feel threatened as teachers, intellectual snobbery, belief in abstractions as the "true"
education, and quality control considerations are
common concerns in most types of experiential learning. These fears often reach fever pitch when
prior learning is involved, because of the student's
total separation from the college or university
setting during the experience.

Procedural issues often hamper the granting of
credit for prior learning. The costs and time
involved in advising, tutorials or seminars, program planning, evaluation, and clerical support
services are significant (Woods, 1977, pp. 115-117).
The participating university must address faculty
load questions, the establishment of exact procedures, the determination of the number of credits

equivalent to certain experiences, recording procedures, the interdisciplinary or intradepartmental
nature of credits, the fee system, and other issues.

Clearly a policy of credit for prior learning
needs to be established based upon a conscious commitment to the value of prior experience.
Otherwise, prior learning will fail to gain legitimacy within the institution. An institution can
begin to combat attitudinal obstacles by providing
recognition for those involved: by providing monetary benefits, by publicizing the efforts involved,
and by counting in the faculty load time spent on
prior learning advisement and evaluation.
Acceptance can also be generated through the clear
delineation of roles, opportunities for input, and
expectations.

The three methods of evaluation discussed
above all raise issues about the granting of credit
for prior learning. David Trivett identifies several of these issues: the relationship of prior
learning to degree objectives rather than to specific course objectives, the necessity of fairness
in granting one student as much credit as another
for the same experience level, and the determination
of how the value of the college experience itself
can be integrated. Some of the more global questions include: Will the original intent of prior
learning be lost in the race for legitimacy and
regulation? What problems will result if prior
learning credit eventually expands to all three
levels of high school, college, and graduate school
and requires transfer among them (Trivett, 1975,
pp. 18-19)?

Peter Meyer feels that prior learning will
never compare favorably to the regular college
experience until faculty recognize the value-laden
aspects of their own teaching and admit that other
values may be legitimate; recognize that all experiential learning is evaluated subjectively and
thus prior learning should not suffer from an evaluation format more stringent than regular experiential learning; overcome their dislike for their
role as "credentialers"; and cease to refuse prior
credit by claiming that accrediting associations
will not allow them to do otherwise (Meyer in
Trivett, 1975, pp. 17-18).

It should be apparent that much of the controversy surrounding prior credit relates specifically
to the area of assessment. The Council for the
Advancement of Experiential Learning (CAEL) currently dominates the field of assessment of

experiential learning. CAEL's efforts are slowly silencing the criticisms that prior learning is a "credit robbery."

The advantages of validating prior learning are several. Awarding credit represents recognition by higher education that an individual's goals and previous learning experience are strongly related to his formal education. Credit for prior learning is based on the idea that learning is not limited to traditional higher educational settings. Acknowledging prior learning emphasizes outcomes and not time served; thus, there is a clear attempt to recognize more than hurdle-jumping. Encouraging greater diversity in the backgrounds of the students attending a college or university fosters a broadened perspective on lifestyles at an institution; granting credit for prior learning makes greater diversity in student background possible.

A disadvantage of prior learning is that the student's educational objectives may get submerged in a struggle for legitimacy. The credit offered for prior learning is frequently not even granted in recognition of the experience itself, but rather for an examination which is supposed to determine whether the experience is equivalent to a specific course. The criteria for granting such credit are often much more stringent than for the classroom learning (Trivett, 1975, pp. 62-63). Residency requirements may be an obstacle when a substantial number of credits are granted (Woods, 1977, pp. 107-108). Evaluation of credits is time-consuming, and the need for evaluators creates an additional cost burden for the university. When seminars, tutorials, and individual counseling are included, the costs continue to rise. The standards of the institution must be carefully considered so that credits granted for prior learning will be of a quality comparable to that of classroom work.

There are many questions which affect the future use of credit for prior learning. Is it desirable and possible to accomplish on a wide scale what advocates of accepting prior learning seek to do? Will graduate schools accept this credit medium? How cost-effective can such a system be? Will widespread use of prior learning credits threaten the legitimacy of higher education? These questions notwithstanding, the academic value of prior learning is gradually becoming accepted throughout higher education. The following examples suggest alternative approaches to validating prior learning.

External credit is offered at The Evergreen State College in Olympia, Washington for understanding and learning derived from a student's nonacademic experiences. To receive credit at Evergreen, a student's experience must meet two criteria: first, it must have taken place over at least a one-year period when the student was not enrolled in any type of educational institution. In addition, the credit cannot be a duplicate of credit received through transfer, CLEP scores, or other means. The institution emphasizes writing as a way to present the experience for evaluation and requires each student seeking external credit to prepare a document for review by the External Credit Review Committee of the College. This committee consists of four faculty members, one student, and one staff member.

The External Credit Office is a group of faculty consultants who assist students in the preparation of the descriptive documents. Student documents must demonstrate: 1) that the student had a nonacademic experience of some sort, from which he learned something similar to what is ordinarily learned for credit in college; 2) that he understands what he has learned; and 3) that the learning and understanding grew out of the experience.

The following quotation, taken from the report which guides the work of the Committee, indicates the emphasis placed on "learning" when awarding credit:

> We conclude that Evergreen should not give credit for experience or skills themselves, but rather for demonstrating understanding: conscious, conceptual, verbal understanding. Operationally, this means explaining and communicating what the person knows so that someone else who doesn't understand it can do so. This seems to us one of the main functions of learning and college, and one of the main things people need in the rest of their lives. And when someone's experience, skill, or knowledge is put in the form of conscious verbal understanding--an extended paper or report-- then it becomes feasible for a committee to make a fair decision about how much college credit to give [The Evergreen State College, n.d.].

Using this criterion, credit has been awarded for such things as photographic skills, day care, human service work, teaching, library work, and computer

162

programming.

The student must apply for external credit during his first quarter at the College, when he must be a registered student. As soon as the student applies, an External Credit Office consultant is assigned to assist him. Due to a limited capacity, only fifteen students may ask for review in a one-quarter period. A completed document must be turned in within three quarters after application is made; however, if the initial credit request is rejected, the document may be rewritten and submitted a total of three times. A student can receive four-, eight-, or twelve-quarter units for the experience. Regardless of the number of external credits granted, the student must complete a minimum of twelve units of credit at Evergreen to receive a B.A. from the institution.

San Francisco State University in California grants credit for prior learning through its Credit by Evaluation for Experiential Learning (CEEL) program. Students petition for academic credit through the General Studies Office, and may gain units in any one of six categories: basic subjects, natural sciences, social sciences, humanities and arts, senior integrative seminar, or optional electives.

Any student wishing to participate must attend a seminar meeting explaining the CEEL program. The seminars are scheduled every two weeks on different days and at a variety of times to accommodate participants' needs. The student chooses a faculty member from among those involved in the program to assist him on an individual basis, and provides the General Studies Office with a petition for credit, an unofficial SFSU transcript, and an Advanced Standing Evaluation form. The student then plans and assembles his portfolio, seeing the faculty member as needed. After assessment of the completed portfolio, the faculty evaluator provides a written description for the student's permanent record and awards credit for the experience.

In both examples faculty participation in the preparation of the written document or portfolio is an essential step in the process. Review at The Evergreen State College is a team effort, while at San Francisco State University credits are evaluated by a single faculty member. Both institutions may grant more or less credit than the amount petitioned for by the student.

Individual Growth and Development Experiences

The purpose of individual growth and development experiences is to enhance a student's personal development and self-examination capacity. Two general types of experiences are included within this category. The first focuses on growth through confrontation with nature and is most commonly referred to as outdoor living programs. Such programs emphasize coping with stress. The second approach to individual development involves experiences in which the individual is explicitly trying to expand certain dimensions of his personality or talents. For example, a student might concentrate on the development of poetic talents, work for a silversmith, or try to learn the art of woodworking to reach a greater understanding of his talents.

Outdoor Living Programs. Prescott College gained a national reputation for its freshmen orientation which culminated in a three-day survival task. The Prescott program sought to develop the examination of one's personal strengths and weaknesses under stress. Outward Bound and the National Outdoor Leadership School are nonuniversity examples of this type of program, which seek to foster interpersonal and personal growth in a variety of geographical and natural settings (e.g., Maine, North Carolina, Wyoming, Africa). The programs vary enough to allow the participant to choose the primary activity: white-water canoeing, mountain climbing, hiking, glacier exploration, sailing, camping, and so on. In most cases, the culminating experience in the search for self-awareness is solo survival. The individual meshes his self-understanding and outdoor techniques in this segment of the experience. Some may just learn a new camping or hiking skill or expand on an old skill. Ideally, however, the experience means learning one's capacity for achievement and risk and how to deal with that knowledge when one returns home. In a few cases, there may be academic discipline objectives attached, as in courses which provide directed study of biology or ecology. Some experiences offer continuing education credit while others, directly related to a university curriculum, may offer physical education or elective credit.

The advantages of outdoor living courses include not only the acquisition of recreation skills but hopefully the development of a deeper self-understanding which can in the future help to

164

integrate the person within both the academic setting and the larger world. The programs offer unusual opportunities to learn about group relationships under stress and the interdependence of group members. When coursework in biology or other disciplines is added, students have the advantage of learning a discipline in the natural setting.

A disadvantage to the student is the high cost often associated with participation, especially in privately-run programs. University programs offered through the physical education department, the student union, student organizations, or other departments usually attempt to keep costs at a reasonable level, although expenses for equipment, transportation, and trained staff may make extensive outdoor living programs prohibitive for university sponsorship. Still, many institutions have been able to offer such programs without placing a heavy financial burden on students or institutional resources.

Clearly, colleges should not attempt to offer such experiences unless their staff is highly skilled in the techniques of wilderness survival and able to cope with the personal and interpersonal dimensions of the experiences. When academic subject matter is added to the experience, selection of instructors becomes another critical factor, especially because it is easy to overlook the student's educational goals in the exhilaration of the experience. Finally, evaluation of learning is difficult since only the skill components are easily measured, while the affective components are difficult to evaluate.

Individual Enrichment Programs. Programs for individual enrichment represent one of the most unique and individualized forms of experiential education. Arthur Chickering mentions one experience of a young man working toward a B.A. in the "Ecology of Integral Being" who combined the art of woodworking and the agricultural skill of pruning trees into a contract learning experience (Chickering, 1977, pp. 30-32). Other experiences might include a search for inner peace through the study of yoga, an analysis of organic farming techniques through working on a farm using these methods, an understanding of documentary photography through living in a small town and doing a pictorial study, or learning how to build a house at the Shelter Institute in Maine. Although an experience may be a means to perfect or to learn skills that are quite tangible, it also has creative and

165

individualistic overtones. Many times individual
enrichment experiences involve journals, portfolios
of work specimens, personal insights, contemporary
readings, and contract learning. Advantages of
such experiences are that the programs are highly
individualized, emphasize the whole person, and
enhance motivation, and that the experiences often
assume a lifetime importance.

Many times it is difficult to evaluate individual enrichment programs for credit; the tangible
outcomes such as photographs are measurable, but
the amount of personal growth is not easily quanti-
fied. Because of the combination of affective and
cognitive growth, it is difficult to assign individual enrichment credits to a specific course in
the curriculum. When programs are travel-oriented,
costs may be high and supervision from a distance
can become difficult; the student may also find
that his best intentions to write journal entries,
to read selected books, or to write reports become
secondary to the experience itself (Chickering,
1977, p. 35).

Both outdoor living and individual enrichment
programs are attractive to college students, primarily because of their emphasis on personal growth.
Further, a sense of adventure tends to surround
these forms of experiential learning and lures the
student who is seeking a different educational component. The personalization of the programs is
perhaps the essence of experiential learning. On
the other hand, such programs are often unclear in
the areas of the assessment of credit and legitimacy. Several short examples suggest some of the
possibilities for developing individual growth
experiences.

Since 1969 Wheaton College in Wheaton, Illinois
has been offering a precollege course named
VANGUARDS at its Northwoods Campus near Three Lakes,
Wisconsin. Separate VANGUARDS courses are offered
for freshman men and women; they are applied toward
the general physical education requirement or the
physical education major.

VANGUARDS essentially uses the many challenges
that occur in the wilderness as a vehicle to provide the optimum environment for group and individual growth. Students gain the skills and knowledge
that enable them to move safely through and live
with the wilderness, its water, mountains, and
forests. As a member of a closely knit group of
ten to twelve, students are prepared for confrontation with themselves and with the elements and

wilderness. Students learn about ropes, condition-
ing, drown proofing, first aid, map reading, and
canoeing, and take short pack trips. In addition,
VANGUARDS provides time for reflection, discussion
of required readings, and journal keeping. The
prime test of the three-week program is a twelve-
day expedition which includes canoeing, backpacking,
a three-day solo, rappelling, a service project, and
a ten-mile marathon at the base camp. In addition
to the VANGUARDS program, Wheaton is actively
involved in a full schedule of other leadership and
outdoor training seminars.

Project Summit at Appalachian State University
in Boone, North Carolina takes a year-round college-
wide approach to wilderness survival. Essentially,
the Project Summit course is a series of varied
challenges in the wilderness or on the sea.

The required portions of Project Summit are
scheduled on weekends during each semester, with a
final expedition of six to eight days scheduled
after the term. Four semester hours of graduate or
undergraduate elective credit are available under
the program. While in the course, each student is
assigned to a crew of ten or twelve members.
Project Summit charges a fee for the academic
credit, provides equipment free of charge, and asks
crew members to provide transportation and food.

The basic block for the course includes afternoon labs equivalent to seven days' work in basic
skills such as rock climbing, rappelling, orien-
teering, cold environs, and survival. Also included
in the basic block are a three-day mountain expedition, a three-day water expedition, and a one-day
service component. Thus, the total time spent in
the basic block is fourteen days. An advanced block
includes a two-day solo period and a six-day marathon experience. The latter takes place during
vacations or the summer and may be either the
college-sponsored challenge or a problem contracted
between the student, professional programs around
the country, and the college office.

ISSUES IN EXPERIENTIAL LEARNING

The preceding discussion has focused on the
definition and elaboration of five categories of
experiential learning. The discussion would be
incomplete, however, without returning to the overall spectrum of experiential learning and identifying the major issues surrounding it. Each type of

167

experiential learning--whether work-learning,
service-learning, cross-cultural experiences, academic credit for prior learning, or individual
growth and development--has its own disadvantages
and advantages to be considered, but experiential
learning as a whole involves issues encompassing
all of these categories. Three main issues pertaining to experiential learning are: its compatibility
with liberal education, the costs related to its
implementation, and the assessment of experiences.

Issue 1: Is Experiential Learning Compatible with the Concept of Liberal Education?

Experiential learning has been criticized by
those who do not see the innovation as consonant
with the goals of undergraduate education. Sidney
Hook, a leading critic of experiential learning,
focuses on the misinterpretations of John Dewey's
conception of experiential learning. He criticizes
the current implementation of experiential learning
as indiscriminate and accepting of all "doing" as
"learning." According to Hook, the question of
what should and should not be accepted as learning
is legitimate and deserves direct attention (Hook,
1971, pp. 22-26). Proponents of experiential
learning do address such criticisms, and are making
extensive efforts to identify and assess educational
experiences.

If experiential learning is accepted as a
legitimate means of education, the question of compatibility with liberal education poses the more
difficult problem of what is meant by liberal education. As has been suggested earlier, revision of
the concept of liberal education has been deemed
essential by many in order that higher education
may be responsive to the needs of a modern society.
In the past, education has excluded most ties to
work and service except at the professional school
level. In the last decade, however, many institutions have redefined liberal education to include
experiential learning components. According to proponents of this new synthesis, when one views education in its broadest and most liberal sense, experiential learning fits naturally with liberal education. Robert Sexton and Richard Ungerer (1975)
explicate the manner in which liberal education is
often merged with experiential learning:

> As a liberal arts education style . . . experi-
> ential education is seen as nonstatic,

sensitizing, utilitarian, and producing autonomy. It is designed to prepare students to
confront a changing world with skills and
attitudes fostered by a liberal arts education
and honed in real endeavors, and a firm sense
of personal well-being. It is seen as contributing to attitudes that help the student relate
to the human experience [pp. 10-11].

William O'Connell and W. Edmund Moomaw encourage educators to think not in terms of particular
majors or courses but rather in terms of the broad
purposes of education; it is in this framework that
one recognizes experiential learning as a complement to and not a substitute for the classroom process of liberal education (O'Connell and Moomaw in
Duley, 1974, p. 89). John Stephenson and Robert
Sexton suggest that in the face of threats to liberal education, experiential learning can be a
"revitalizing force." This renewal can come through
providing the student with increased sensitivity to
and understanding of the human condition, and
especially through the interaction of humanistic
reflection and active involvement (Stephenson and
Sexton, 1974, pp. 12-26). While others are less
sanguine about the possibilities of relating experiential learning to the liberal arts, there is widespread sentiment that the distinctions between the
two can and should be broken down.

Issue 2: What Are the Costs Related to Implementing Experiential Learning?

Any college which accepts experiential learning as a desirable means to accomplish its mission
must also carefully consider the costs involved in
such a commitment. The level of costs may vary
with: 1) the structural level of the activity;
2) the number of categories of experiential learning implemented; and 3) the scope of each category.
Commitment may be less than institutional, center-
ing only within a department or within a school;
for example, modern language majors may be the only
students involved in credited foreign study, or the
School of Business Administration may be the only
segment of the institution to support internships.
Only one or two of the five possible categories of
experiential learning might be instituted. A college might support only academic credit for prior
learning or individual growth and development.
Finally, the scope of the experience may be as

broad or as limited as desired: all students might
be required to participate, or a single academic
class might be allowed to enter into the experience.

Institutions committed to experiential learning should not be deceived into thinking that focusing on only one or two programs precludes an
institution-wide impact. It is easy to concentrate
only on the obvious costs of coordinating office,
supplies, telephone bills, and brochure printing.
The costs go beyond budgeted dollars, however, to
include other institutional resources such as staff
time. It takes time to select the most qualified
director, to advise a student on foreign study, or
to set up job placements.

The impact of establishing experiential learning programs also goes far beyond even time and
dollar costs, however. Institutions must view the
commitment to experiential learning as a major
interpretation of their mission and as having consequences for many areas of the institution.
According to Arthur Chickering, a college needs to
anticipate the possible effects on the areas of
admissions and recruitment; financial aid; advising,
career planning, and personal counseling; student-
faculty ratios; per student costs of educational
facilities and resources; classroom space; dormitory
residency; and administrative costs (Chickering,
1977, pp. 77-78). The adaptation of an institution's mission to include experiential learning
takes on major proportions; institutions cannot
take such a commitment lightly.

Chickering (1977) makes nine suggestions to
universities and colleges wishing to implement
experiential learning, in order to foresee some of
the costs involved:

1. Identify the numbers and kinds of new students likely to enroll and project potential income.
2. Project personnel costs for a director and
   secretary, supplies and expense money
   needed, and travel funds required--includ-
   ing those for students, if necessary.
3. Estimate added costs or savings in recruitment, admissions processes, and materials.
4. Estimate increases or decreases in financial aid requests. Estimate wages and sti-
   pends available from various experiential
   learning settings. Estimate potential
   sources of support from unions, businesses,
   social agencies, and the like.

5. Estimate costs for additional staff, time, and scheduling changes to provide educational advising and personal counseling.
6. Specify anticipated student-faculty ratios. If they are higher or lower than ratios for current alternatives, estimate the differences in savings or costs.
7. Estimate consequences for space utilization including laboratories, seminar rooms, and lounges for small group meetings as well as classrooms.
8. Estimate consequences for residential facilities and food services and calculate differences in income and expenses.
9. Estimate costs associated with extra time, travel, and secretarial services for administrators other than the director [p. 78].

Presently there is no handy reference manual for administrators to use in estimating these costs. They must rely on the suggestions of others at similar institutions which have tried to implement programs.

Issue 3: What Assessment Issues Must Be Addressed to Assure Legitimacy and Quality in Experiential Learning?

Educators are concerned that careful evaluation be given to experiential learning in order to avoid the possibility of the indiscriminate acceptance of all experiences for academic credit. Innovators in the field have begun to make some progress toward the resolution of these evaluation concerns. At the national level, CAEL has sponsored many such efforts through publications, newsletters, and workshops aimed at developing and refining tools and techniques for assessment.

Although the specific evaluation questions may differ, the general concern with evaluative data is common to all five categories of experiential learning. For the institution involved in work- and service-learning programs, the concern is twofold: first, evaluation of the setting and duties performed to ensure valuable learning opportunities as well as work or service experience, and second, evaluation of student performance according to standards acceptable to both the institution and the employer. On-site visits by faculty, employer supervision, final project papers from students, and seminars are examples of the techniques used to assess work- and service-learning. For the cross-cultural experience, colleges may utilize pre- and post-seminars, evaluation of catalog descriptions, and student journals. The assessment criteria for prior learning may include portfolios, test scores, skills demonstrations, or individual advising. The individual growth and development experience may include the evaluation of specific skills, journals, completed readings, discussions of the experience, and leader opinions.

Despite the diversity in the techniques utilized, different programs all attempt to evaluate what the student has gained from the experience in light of stated educational goals. Assessment is particularly difficult because information and skill acquisition are seldom the only learning goals; personal growth and affective learning are often additional goals, but they are especially difficult to evaluate. How does one measure the personal awareness developed during stress in the wilderness? How can one measure the ability to understand a different culture or subculture? Or should one evaluate only proficiency in French or expertise at rappelling and simply avoid the affective dimensions?

Experiential learning is an innovation which tries to recognize student educational goals as well as goals of the college. A key problem is how to order these goals and weight them in the assessment process. The architecture student who builds his own house sees the application of design principles and theory as secondary to the actual experience of utilizing the theory and building a house which is structurally sound. Is the experience judged by the student's ability to expound upon design principles, on the time spent, or on its structural soundness when completed? At what point are his initiative and pride in completion considered?

Finally, an institution must decide how to credit an experience once it is deemed legitimate. Should it be a pass/fail evaluation or should a letter grade be assigned? At what level should the experience be credited: is it equivalent to a specific course, does it meet a general education requirement, or is it an elective? The type of credit given and the division of the institution from which it comes say a great deal about the commitment and attitude of the institution toward experiential learning.

Each of these issues should be confronted by institutions considering innovation in undergraduate

education. The first issue, which poses the question of the compatibility of traditional liberal
education with experiential learning, requires a
thoughtful institutional response. Although there
are persuasive arguments in favor of increasing
experiential learning opportunities, institutions
must evaluate potential programs in light of
institutionally-shared conceptions of undergraduate
education. Assuming that an institution embraces
a philosophy of education which includes experiential learning, many hard questions about implementation and assessment remain to be answered. The
institutional implications are likely to be substantial, and planning cannot be an overnight affair.
Yet, as this chapter attempts to document, a wide
range of colleges and universities is seeking in a
variety of ways to make experiential learning a
larger component of the undergraduate experience.

REFERENCES

Brick, Michael, and Earl J. McGrath. _Innovations
    in Liberal Arts Colleges_. New York: Teachers
    College Press, Columbia University, 1969.
The Carnegie Foundation for the Advancement of
    Teaching. _Missions of the College Curriculum_.
    San Francisco: Jossey-Bass, 1977.
Chickering, Arthur W. "Developmental Change as a
    Major Outcome." In Morris T. Keeton and
    Associates, _Experiential Learning: Rationale_,
    Characteristics, and Assessment. San
    Francisco: Jossey-Bass, 1976: 62-107.
Chickering, Arthur W. _Experience and Learning: An
    Introduction to Experiential Learning_. New
    Rochelle, New York: Change Magazine Press,
    1977.
Cohen, Gail (ed.). _Summer Study Abroad_. New York:
    Institute of International Education, 1978.
Coleman, James S. "Differences between Experiential
    and Classroom Learning." In Morris T. Keeton
    and Associates, _Experiential Learning:
    Rationale, Characteristics, and Assessment_.
    San Francisco: Jossey-Bass, 1976: 49-61.
Cross, K. Patricia. _The Integration of Learning
    and Earning: Cooperative Education and
    Nontraditional Study_. ERIC/Higher Education
    Research Report No. 4. Washington, D.C.:
    American Association for Higher Education,
    1973.

Davis, James R. "Cooperative Education: Prospects and Pitfalls." Journal of Higher Education, 43 (1972): 139-146.

Dewey, John. The School and Society. Chicago: University of Chicago Press, 1915.

Dressel, Paul L. College and University Curriculum. 2nd ed. Berkeley, California: McCutchan, 1971.

Duley, John. "Cross-Cultural Field Study." In John Duley (ed.), Implementing Field Experience Education: New Directions for Higher Education. San Francisco: Jossey-Bass, 1974: 13-21.

Eberly, Donald J. "Service-Learning: the Road Ahead." National Service Newsletter (1974): 2.

Educational Testing Service. Testing Programs, Special Services, Instructional Activities at Educational Testing Service. Princeton, New Jersey: Educational Testing Service, 1970.

Goodwyn, H. Merrill, Jr. "Guidelines for Further Development and Expansion of the Texas Service-Learning Program." In Service-Learning in the South. Atlanta, Georgia: Southern Regional Educational Board, 1973: 32-43.

Gordon, Sheila C. "Campus and Workplace as Arenas." In Morris T. Keeton and Associates, Experiential Learning: Rationale, Characteristics, and Assessment. San Francisco: Jossey-Bass, 1976: 108-118.

Hofer, Barbara, Robert F. Sexton, and Ernest Yanarella. "Exploring the Psycho-Political Development of Liberal Arts Interns." In Initiating Experiential Learning Programs: Four Case Studies. Princeton, New Jersey: Cooperative Assessment of Experiential Learning, 1976: 167-219.

Hook, Sidney. "John Dewey and His Betrayers." Change, 3 (1971): 22-26.

Houle, Cyril O. "Deep Traditions of Experiential Learning." In Morris T. Keeton and Associates, Experiential Learning: Rationale, Characteristics, and Assessment. San Francisco: Jossey-Bass, 1976: 19-33.

Hyink, Bernard L. Focus on Cooperative Education. Fullerton, California: Trustees of the California State University and Colleges, 1977.

Jarrell, Donald W. "Professional Development: Get Them Early." Training in Business and Industry, 2 (1974).

Keeton, Morris T. "Credentials for the Learning
    Society." In Morris T. Keeton and Associates,
    Experiential Learning: Rationale,
    Characteristics, and Assessment. San
    Francisco: Jossey-Bass, 1976: 1-18.
Magill, Samuel H. "The Aims of Liberal Education
    in the Post-Modern World." Liberal Education,
    63 (1977): 435-442.
O'Connell, William R., Jr. "Service-Learning as a
    Strategy for Innovation in Undergraduate
    Instruction." In Service-Learning in the
    South. Atlanta, Georgia: Southern Regional
    Education Board, 1973: 4-7.
Olson, Paul A. Concepts of Career and General
    Education. ERIC/Higher Education Research
    Report No. 8. Washington, D.C.: American
    Association for Higher Education, 1977.
Rudolph, Frederick. The American College and
    University: A History. New York: Vintage,
    1962.
Sexton, Robert F., and Richard A. Ungerer.
    Rationales for Experiential Education. ERIC/
    Higher Education Research Report No. 3.
    Washington, D.C.: American Association for
    Higher Education, 1975.
Sigmon, Robert L. A Notebook on Service Learning.
    Raleigh, North Carolina: Internship Office,
    October, 1972.
Sigmon, Robert L. "Service-Learning in North
    Carolina." In John Duley (ed.), Implementing
    Field Experience Education: New Directions
    for Higher Education. San Francisco: Jossey-
    Bass, 1974: 23-30.
Society for Field Experience Education and the
    National Center for Public Service Internship
    Programs. Newsletter. Washington, D.C.:
    September/October, 1977.
Stephenson, John B., and Robert F. Sexton.
    "Experiential Education and the Revitalization
    of the Liberal Arts." In Sidney Hook, Paul
    Kurtz, and Miro Todorovich (eds.), The
    Philosophy of the Curriculum: The Need for
    General Education. Buffalo, New York:
    Prometheus, 1975: 12-26.
Student Advisory Committee, Council on International
    Education Exchange. Guidelines on Developing
    Campus Services for Students Going Abroad.
    New York: Council on International Educational
    Exchange, 1973.

Trivett, David A. Academic Credit for Prior Off-Campus Learning. ERIC/Higher Education Research Report No. 2. Washington, D.C.: American Association for Higher Education, 1975.

Tumin, Melvin. "Valid and Invalid Rationales." In Morris T. Keeton and Associates, Experiential Learning: Rationale, Characteristics, and Assessment. San Francisco: Jossey-Bass, 1976: 41-48.

Winkie, Joy D. "Responsibility and Cooperative Education." In Charles W. Havice (ed.), Campus Values. New York: Charles Scribner's Sons, 1971: 133-144.

Woods, James A. "Evaluating Life Experiences: Current Practices at the Collegiate Level." Alternative Higher Education, 2 (1977): 105-118.

6
Calendar and Degree Innovations*

Many colleges and universities have recently begun to experiment with ways to provide flexibility in two major structural features of the college curriculum: the calendar and the degree requirements. Unlike many of the other kinds of innovations already discussed, changes in these structural variables have a direct impact throughout the entire undergraduate experience. Because of their comprehensive nature, these changes may actually foster, as well as complement, innovation in other curricular areas.

Innovations in calendar and degree programs are usually intended to increase the time, space, and decision options open to students. Existing time and requirement patterns, which have been based as much on tradition as on any educational objective, are now being made more sensitive to student needs.

To the traditional division of the academic year into quarters and semesters have been added many new arrangements. The first section of this chapter looks at the diversification of the college calendar and the move toward intensive terms. The second section of the chapter discusses three types of new degree structures: accelerated degrees, external degrees, and student-designed programs. By way of introduction, it is useful to see if there are any discernible trends in the history of the development of new academic calendars.

---

*Jean Wyer Hatcher assumed major responsibility for chapter six.

A BRIEF HISTORY OF THE COLLEGE CALENDAR

The colonial college offered a single course
of study to all students. Henry Dunster, an early
president of Harvard College, described the curriculum he brought from Cambridge in eleven words:

Primus annus Rhetoricam docebit, secundus et
tertius Dialecticam, quartus adiungat
Philosophiam. [The first year will teach
rhetoric; the second and third dialectic; the
fourth will add philosophy.] [Earnest, 1953,
p. 20].

All students followed the same curriculum, and
classes were small enough that scheduling for an
entire college was no different than scheduling for
a single student. Despite attempts to make meaningful changes in the course of study through the
introduction of new subjects, the rigidity of the
colonial curriculum prevailed until well into the
nineteenth century. The year after the Yale Report
of 1828, that college presented its entire bachelor
course of study on a single page of its catalogue
(Schmidt, 1957, p. 56).

The curricular variety which requires attention to the design, content, and scheduling of
courses did not appear until the late nineteenth
century. As the classical tradition experienced
horizontal and vertical expansion through the development of professional and graduate schools, the
degree program options available to students
expanded. At the same time, the development of the
elective system broke the lockstep comparability of
undergraduate liberal arts curricula. As the curriculum expanded and student options increased,
colleges and universities developed administrative
mechanisms to match students and instruction. A
system of courses and credits evolved to allow work
in disparate fields of study to be equated for certification purposes. Laurence Veysey (1965) notes
that Harvard initiated assembly line registration
in 1891 and moved on to a perforated card system in
1896. He observes that

At most universities, courses were . . . ra-
tionalized into a numerical system of units for
credit; the catalogue began to resemble the
inventory of a well-stocked and neatly labeled
general store [p. 312].

178

Variety in term arrangements was as slow to develop as were formalized course structures. Not only did the early college student work long hours every day, but he was also allowed little relief through vacations. The only major interruption was a long break in the spring. The rest of the year was broken into four terms, following the British model. This arrangement came under fire in the early nineteenth century. George Ticknor argued that "the longest vacation should happen in the hot season, when insubordination and misconduct are now most frequent, partly from the indolence produced by the season [Hofstadter and Smith, 1961, p. 271]." The first, greatest, and most lasting change in the collegiate calendar accomplished what Ticknor proposed, but for very different reasons. The advent of the semester calendar shifted the long vacation to the summer and broke the academic year into two equal terms. It was adopted, not for academic reasons, but rather to accommodate the work patterns of an agrarian economy. This term structure has long outlasted the social structure that shaped it. According to Loyd Oleson, 83 percent of the country's colleges still operated on a "traditional semester" calendar in the late 1960s (Chronicle of Higher Education, January 16, 1978, p. 13).

In the late nineteenth century, summer again became an active academic period with the development of institutes for teachers and farmers. Harvard offered the first regular summer term in 1869 as part of a program which sent its students to teach in the lower schools during the winter term. Although it is difficult to state precisely when the year-round calendar began, its roots are found in the summer school movement (Davis, 1972, p. 143). At least in part, the acceptance of the summer term as an equal in the academic calendar came with the inclusion of the four-quarter calendar in the original plan for the University of Chicago in 1892. The quarter system continues to be popular, running second to the semester calendar in the number of schools in which it is used.

In recent years, some institutions on the semester systems have responded to pressure for full summer terms by adding a full summer semester. The resulting three-semester (or "trimester") yearlong calendar became quite popular during the 1960s.

The first major departure from terms of equal duration was the development of the "interim" term or 4-1-4 calendar. Sandwiched between two equal

179

long terms during which students often take four
courses is a month-long term devoted to intensive
work on a single subject. This calendar was first
adopted by Eckerd College (then Florida
Presbyterian) in 1959. Since then, over 300 colleges have adopted some form of the short term
calendar.

RECENT TRENDS IN CALENDAR ARRANGEMENTS

A survey of 2,472 institutions, conducted in
1976 by Loyd Oleson (Chronicle of Higher Education,
January 16, 1978, p. 13), found the following distribution of calendar types:

Calendar Type	Number	%
Traditional Semester	172	7
Early Semester	1,172	48
Quarter	586	24
Trimester	86	3
4-1-4	324	13
Other	132	5

Clearly the semester and quarter patterns are still
predominant. However, an interesting change has
recently taken place within the semester framework.
While maintaining the integrity of the term structure, most semester-based institutions have shifted
the starting date from mid-September to late August
to allow completion of the first semester before
the Christmas recess. This serves the educational
purpose of temporally integrating the first semester, and combines the traditional Christmas vacation
and intersession recess. Combining the vacations
reduces student travel costs and may also reduce
heating and overhead costs.
Of the institutions, 18 percent reported one
of the nontraditional categories: 4-1-4 or Other.
Innovative work in calendar design usually involves
the use of the interim term or adoption of the modular calendar. The major trend in calendar variations is toward the examination, definition, and
increased use of "intensive" rather than "concurrent" terms. Several of the more interesting variations will be discussed in more detail in the next
section.

NEW CALENDAR VARIATIONS

The critical factor in evaluating any calendar arrangement is the extent to which its scheduling options offer flexibility, for both time and space flexibility are important in meeting educational goals. Time decisions should be sensitive to student learning rates, instructor's preferences, and subject matter characteristics. Space flexibility allows choice of location and is based on the size of the term units and the number of entry/exit points in the calendar.

Designing a calendar involves the treatment of two variables: courses and terms. A course is a predetermined set of learning experiences leading to the award of credit or some other type of certification. A term is a specified period of time in which one or more courses are taken. The most important factor in designing the college calendar is the relationship between courses and terms. The more traditional approach is to plan long terms during which several courses--usually three, four, or five--are taken concurrently. One emerging alternative is to have students do intensive work in one or two subjects over a much shorter time period. Using names which describe the type of effort required of the student, the former is referred to as a concurrent pattern and the latter as an intensive pattern.

The traditional, and still predominant, semester, quarter, and trimester calendars are concurrent. Under these arrangements, possibilities for matching the pace of instruction to the material being presented are often limited. Faculty have no alternative but to fit the material to a term structure which may have little, if any, relation to the educational objectives of the course. Students are involved in several courses during each term and must spread their efforts over all required tasks. Some minor flexibility is achieved by allowing differences in the credit weights applied to the various courses to provide some correspondence between effort and reward. Examples of this include granting more credit for laboratory courses or less for physical education.

Under the semester or quarter calendar the only way to adjust the pace of a course is to manipulate the amount of material presented within the set term period. Since most courses presented under traditional calendars have evolved over a number of years and are rarely subject to complete

181

reevaluation, the traditional calendar may have difficulty providing sensitivity to students, instructors, or subject matter. Even with some variation in credit, the traditional, concurrent calendar frequently provides little opportunity for the matching of temporal arrangements and educational goals.

Geographic choice is possible under concurrent calendars, but the length of the term and the size of the course load limit space flexibility to major learning commitments. For a student at a "semester" institution to be away from campus, the off-campus opportunity must represent at least one eighth of his undergraduate experience. This works well with "transient" terms at other colleges or in established programs geared to the traditional calendar (semester or year abroad programs), but it does not allow for the inclusion of briefer or less structured opportunities.

A major advantage of the traditional calendar is its credibility. It is well-known and understood, and therefore, unless significantly challenged, will remain the norm. Students with semester or quarter transcripts encounter few credit accounting difficulties when transferring to another school or meeting certification requirements. Semester and quarter hours are the accepted coinage of the credit market.

Innovation in the use of traditional calendar options is difficult to accomplish. Beyond the time and space constraints discussed above, the calendar suffers from the inertia of an existing, accepted term structure. Not only can this dampen any attempt at changing the calendar itself, it may also hamper innovation in other areas.

The development of intensive calendar patterns is a response to growing dissatisfaction with arbitrary temporal patterns and represents an effort to match term structure to learning experiences. Recognition that the concurrent calendar could provide neither optimal scheduling patterns for some existing courses nor opportunities for innovation in course design led to the development of the 4-1-4 or "interim" calendar.

The interim calendar uses the single intensive term as an alternative to the long, concurrent sessions. Courses may be taught in one or both of the time frames. By releasing the participants from the fragmented efforts of the concurrent terms, the intensive term is designed to provide a new option for meeting student and faculty needs.

182

While there were a few attempts at calendar innovation prior to the 4-1-4, these were generally short-lived or scattered among developing institutions. The interim calendar was the first nontraditional calendar with lasting and broad impact. The effects of the interim term went far beyond the expectations for a calendar modification.

> The changed circumstances of the one month period, the single-minded attention to just one project, and the increased use of nontraditional subject matter brought about unanticipated consequences. Student initiative in planning and carrying through academic work as independent study, a changing teacher role and a vitalized teaching/learning relationship, the experience of intensive learning--all signified fundamental change and reform [Association for Innovation in Higher Education, 1974, p. 1].

The short term is especially helpful in allowing for space flexibility. For this one term, the risk of experimenting is much less than for a whole semester or quarter. Students can use the interim period for off-campus study with less disruption and for a smaller part of their total undergraduate experience. Disruption of the on-campus experience is minimized because of the short length of the term and the relatively high number of students who take advantage of the opportunity to work off-campus. One drawback of the interim calendar is that its flexible term is usually only available once during the year and may not coincide with a desired opportunity.

Although there is little research on the effectiveness of the intensive term, 4-1-4 calendars are fairly well accepted. The Association for Innovation in Higher Education was founded in 1970 as the "4-1-4 Conference." This consortium of schools using the interim has stimulated interest in the calendar form and publishes information concerning a variety of off-campus and foreign-based programs.

As any listing of interim course offerings indicates, the short term has increased the use of nontraditional subject matter and off-campus learning experiences. The important question is whether this leads to meaningful innovation in the rest of the curriculum. David Halliburton argues that because the interim term becomes a focus for

innovation, it "short-circuits" more comprehensive
change, "leaving the conventional curriculum to go
grinding along at its usual glacial pace
[Halliburton, 1977, p. 68]." On the other hand,
the frustrations and the rewards of dealing with
the interim may pave the way for more radical
change.

Recognition of the beneficial effects of the
single intensive interim term has led to efforts to
extend these benefits throughout the academic year
by breaking the long four-course terms into intensive terms using modular calendars. Significantly,
the rationale underlying the modular calendar goes
beyond the need for flexibility, met through a
single innovative term, that is associated with the
4-1-4 calendar. Rather, the modular calendar is
based on a belief that the intensive pattern best
accommodates most or all learning experiences.

Modular calendars break the nine-month academic year into four or more terms, called modules,
of equal or different lengths. Courses which
require a longer term can be scheduled across several modules. Alternatively, one term can be
totally devoted to intensive study of a single
topic. A half-term option allows learning units to
be broken down into even smaller components, providing for the inclusion of topics which are not
suited to a full-length module. In contrast to
traditional calendars, increased scheduling options
provide considerable flexibility in matching learning rates and temporal arrangements. Implementation
of the modular calendar may be achieved by adapting
the existing curriculum to the new schedule or by
the more radical approach of designing a totally
new curriculum.

Modular calendars, especially those combining
four or more terms with double or half weighting
courses, provide many choices for pacing material.
This flexibility allows increased fidelity between
course scheduling and both internal and external
needs. Not only are student and faculty desires
more easily accommodated, but the modular calendar
is more easily tailored to a variety of off-campus
learning experiences. The increased number of
entry/exit dates also allows more options for students entering the program.

There are two primary criticisms of the modular program. First is that the intensive course
work sets a pace which is too exhausting over the
whole year. While fewer courses over shorter terms
seem to be a welcome relief from the competing

demands of concurrent calendars, the rapid succession of short, concentrated terms is not the perfect answer to the problem of calendar design. The second criticism of the modular calendar is the frequency of disruptions for course changes. This can be partially mitigated by holding one or two registration sessions a year, each covering several modules.

The modular calendar is the newest and most diverse term arrangement. It is still in the development stage, and there has been little real effort to evaluate it. General acceptance of the educational validity of the calendar has yet to be proven.

One of the pioneering programs in the development of modular calendars is the Colorado College "block plan" approach, which divides the calendar into nine blocks of three and one-half weeks. Each block is followed by a break of four and one-half days. A block is worth three and one-half semester hours, or one unit of credit. Students normally take one principal course during each block. Most courses fill one block, though some fill two or three.

Another approach to developing a modular calendar is to divide the academic year into four equal terms. In 1973, Stephens College adopted a calendar of this type employing seven-week terms. The plan was modeled after the modular calendar at Colorado College but allows a greater number of concurrent registrations. Students can enroll for two or two and one-half courses per term. The calendar change was implemented in conjunction with the adoption of an accelerated degree program. The task of redesigning individual courses was left up to faculty members and there were some problems. However, the faculty have recently reaffirmed their support of the modular calendar, which "seems to have accomplished at least several of its objectives . . . and overcome some of the most glaring problems."*

A similar split of long concurrent terms into two equal short terms is the basis for Muskingum College's "Octal" calendar, introduced in the 1978-1979 academic year. Each traditional sixteen-week

---

*Personal communication with the Dean of the Faculty, December 14, 1977.

semester is divided into two eight-week terms
called "octals." The basic student load is two
courses and one or more units per term. (A unit is
equal to one fourth of a course, with thirty-one
courses and twelve units required for graduation.)
A regular course may be extended to cover two modules or compressed into half a module. The combination of units and long, short, and regular courses
provides the instructor with a wide choice of temporal arrangements, yet allows for the use of uni-
form blocks for scheduling ease.

The Octal calendar is designed to provide

. . . a continuity and rhythm to the learning
year that is uninterrupted by the intellectual
hibernation period many faculty associate with
the combined Christmas break and January
Interim . . . . Closely related is provision
for optimal use of facilities (buildings,
heating, food service, etc.) during a solid
(but shortened) academic year [Muskingum
College: Prospectus, 1976, p. 17].

As the Muskingum Prospectus explains, another
reason for adopting the modular calendar is that it
"will lead all faculty members to rethink what they
are doing, how they are doing it, and perhaps to
decide to do new things in new ways [Muskingum
College: Prospectus, 1976, p. 17]." The availability of a variety of term design options and the
need to adjust to the new calendar should stimulate
the examination of existing curricular practices
and the development of new ones.

Unlike the Stephens and Muskingum plans, which
utilize terms of equal length, Ottawa University
operates on a 2-2-1-2-2 academic year augmented by
two short, optional summer terms. The longer terms,
during which students take two courses, last two
months and the shorter terms are scheduled to last
one month. Ottawa stresses the need for the calendar to complement the curriculum, while at the same
time facilitating internships and off-campus study
through the variety in term lengths and the number
of entry/exit dates. It also allows students to
graduate early if they enroll for nine four-
semester-hour courses each year.

In summary, the major trend in the development
of new academic calendars is away from traditional
and arbitrary divisions of time and toward temporal
units which attempt to match student need, instructor preferences, and educational goals. The

success of the "interim" calendar, as well as the
recent growth of modular scheduling, may portend a
large-scale move away from traditional concurrent
arrangements toward a wider acceptance of intensive
calendar patterns. Even if a calendar revolution
does not lie in the immediate future, the diversity
of existing calendar arrangements suggests that
many institutions have come to realize the importance of designing temporal patterns which are compatible with their entire curricular program.

NEW DEGREE PROGRAMS

While many of the calendar variations have
attracted widespread attention, these innovations
continue to define education largely in terms of
"time" rather than "learning." Especially in light
of the new kinds of students now enrolled in higher
education, calendar variations do not go far enough
in providing the kind of curricular flexibility
that allows for variability in individual learning.
As a consequence, many new degree programs
have been developed which differ from traditional
degree programs in that they emphasize learning out-
comes--rather than accumulated time-units--as the
basis for a baccalaureate degree. It follows from
this basic premise that traditional conceptions of
the when and where of education need to be expanded,
so the new degree programs also provide more flexible time and space arrangements. Learning can
take place in a variety of settings (off-campus as
well as on-campus) and at a variety of times. Some
of the new programs go even farther by providing
the flexibility of student-designed programs.
There are three major types of new degree programs.
First, accelerated degree programs provide increased
time flexibility for students. Second, external
degree programs add the notion of space flexibility.
Finally, student-designed programs combine time,
space, and program flexibility.

ACCELERATED DEGREE PROGRAMS

Accelerated degree programs offer the option
of time-shortened baccalaureate degrees. They are
primarily targeted at traditional students; although
they may try to reach these students earlier, institutions have made little effort to expand the clientele served by accelerated degree programs. The

187

programs are usually selected by students who have a clear career or graduate school choice, though they also may be selected for reasons of cost reduction. Substantial savings may accrue from reduced tuition and living expenses over the shortened time in college.

There are three major types of accelerated degree programs. Overload programs exist largely through student initiative. To graduate in three years within a standard four-year program, the student takes an overload during the regular academic year and may also take courses in summer school. Unless specifically prohibited, this option can be exercised by anyone willing to carry sufficient hours. Students pursuing an accelerated path within an existing degree have no special institutional programs available for their support. Problems may occur in the availability and sequencing of courses or the acceptance of summer school credit earned at another institution. Little can be said about innovation in overload programs as they are informal, and the creative work is being done by individual students learning to cope with the work load and the scheduling problems.

The second type of accelerated degree program is separate from the regular four-year program. To gain quality control over accelerating students and provide them with specialized support, several institutions have developed a formal acceleration option as an alternative to the traditional four-year degree. Specific declaration and admission requirements are often used to identify qualifying students.

An example of a separate accelerated degree program is the Three-Year Degree at Stephens College. This program and a modular calendar were adopted by the faculty in 1973. Prior to that time, the College had offered an overload accelerated Bachelor of Fine Arts which required three years and two summers of coursework. The new program was a response to several pressures. There was concern not only over the decreasing size of the entering class but also over the quality of the freshman experience.

The College also had concerned itself for some time with what seemed to be a real difficulty in establishing the freshman year as an educational experience representing a clear departure from [the] senior year of high school. Many of [the College's] students reported

188

that work in freshman courses duplicated courses they had taken in secondary school and that, indeed, some of the texts were the same; these students found themselves bored and at loose ends, and some of them left during or after their first year [Stephens College, 1977, p. 61].

In conjunction with "the pervasive flexibility and individualization of the Stephens College Program," the College designed a three-year degree which does not require summer work and which raises the student load during the regular term from two and one-half to three courses. At the same time, the College altered its depth and breadth require- ments. Students must opt for the Three-Year pro- gram early in their college career, plan carefully, and may have to forego some elective courses. They are required to apply separately to the program and must maintain a 2.5 grade average.

During the 1976-77 year, Stephens conducted a review of the Three-Year Degree Program. The review found that although the program does not draw new students to the college, it has encouraged potential transfers to stay. Graduates of the three-year program were found to be as successful in graduate school and the job market as four-year graduates.

Combining the regular curriculum with extra- university learning is the third way to structure an accelerated degree program. Designers of com- bined programs have gone outside the university to assess prior or concurrent learning in other set- tings, often in the secondary schools. As with other accelerated degrees, freshman-year dissatis- faction is often cited as a motivating factor in the development of these programs.

Colleges have been granting credit for second- ary school coursework on an individual course basis for many years. Often the credit was based on sat- isfactory performance on an internally devised achievement test or on one of the College Entrance Examination Board Advanced Placement Tests. Formal programs restructuring the undergraduate degree to maximize the use of prior and concurrent learning are a recent development. Two examples from the State University of New York will be discussed here: the Fredonia 3-1-3 Program which was developed in 1972, and the Geneseo Three-Year Baccalaureate Degree Program, initiated in 1971.

The State University College at Fredonia offers

189

a time-shortened, 3-1-3 program. The numbers refer
to years in an institutional setting rather than
courses per term. Qualified students who have completed three years of high school divide their time
between high school and college during a transitional year. They should then be able to graduate
from college in three more years, reducing the
normal eight-year secondary and higher education
sequence to seven years. During the transitional
year, students enroll in three courses each semester at the college and two courses at their local
high school. After this year, the student should
be able to transfer to another college or continue
at Fredonia as a sophomore. Credit for the high
school work is included, without grades, in the college transcript and the college work is credited
toward the student's high school diploma.

Clearly, the critical factor in designing and
implementing a program of this type is coordination
between the college and the high school. Fredonia
relies on the secondary schools to nominate students
for the program, but it chooses which high school
courses it will accept for credit.

L. Walter Schultze, Director of Institutional
Research at the State University of New York at
Fredonia, states that it was hypothesized that
Fredonia's accelerated program would

> . . . strengthen the present high school year
> by encouraging student enrollment in a full
> academic program and thereby reduce boredom;
> avoid unnecessary duplication of material of
> the senior year of high school and the fresh-
> man year of college; acknowledge the advanced
> nature of some courses in the modern high
> school by giving college credit for such
> courses; improve articulation between the high
> schools and the colleges [Schultze, The 3-1-3
> Experiment: First Annual Report, 1973, p. 2].

In addition to the educational goals expressed
above, the College at Fredonia also intends to
reduce the cost of the total college education, both
to the students and to the state. The primary cost
reduction to the student is the one-time saving
from the transfer of twelve hours of credit from
the high school. Savings from the state standpoint
are harder to quantify, but appear to be significant.

One problem with the program cost is the status
of the high school hours for transfer students.

Since many students use the program as a transition period before transfer to another college, the receiving college's treatment of transfer credits has a heavy impact on the cost reduction to the student. An initial study showed fairly wide acceptance, but the experience of the first transfer group showed that real acceptance rates varied widely.

Students in the 3-1-3 Program are treated as much as possible like regular freshmen during the transition year and seem to blend easily into sophomore cohorts whether at Fredonia or elsewhere. A study of these students after the second year of college concludes that they "were not handicapped in attaining two years of general knowledge in the social sciences, humanities, or natural sciences (Schultze, The 3-1-3 Experiment: The Second Year, 1975, p. 26).

While the Fredonia Program offers students the opportunity for concurrent learning, the State University College at Geneseo offers a program based on prior learning. In its Three-Year Baccalaureate Degree Program, the largest in the SUNY system, Geneseo uses the Undergraduate Area Examinations from the Educational Testing Service. Students must pass proficiency examinations in social science, natural science, and humanities and complete a ninety semester hour program that includes a traditional liberal arts major.

As with the Fredonia Program, avoiding curriculum overlap and reducing costs are the primary motivating factors behind the program. Geneseo has found that its Three-Year graduates have higher grade-point averages and higher Graduate Record Examination Scores than comparable four-year students. In 1976 the institution estimated that a student saved $3,125 by completing the Three-Year Program.

By accepting students equal in age and experience to the normal freshman group and by relying on standardized tests for certifying achievement, Geneseo has developed a time-shortened program which requires a minimum of additional effort on the part of the College. This allows much broader participation in the program. By the third year of operation, the College had dropped all special academic selection criteria and over 60 percent of the freshman class were enrolled in the Three-Year Program (Research Report, 1976, p. 2).

Early exit, which creates both a time-shortened path to a career or graduate school and a reduction in costs to the student and the institution, is the

191

most visible advantage of accelerated degree programs. The opportunity to start work or graduate education, especially in fields requiring lengthy training, can provide the capable, well-motivated student with a meaningful alternative to the traditional four-year sequence. Cost reduction is of concern to a broader range of students; significant savings which can be maintained throughout the degree process are an important advantage for almost any student. Another advantage of many accelerated degree programs is their effect on the freshman year experience. Through more careful examination of students' secondary preparation, time-shortened programs are often instrumental in improving the high school--college interface.

The primary disadvantage of accelerated degree programs is their impact on the finances of the institutions offering them. Many schools, especially those relying on testing for advancement, may experience no increase in net burden from these programs. However, where tuition adjustments do not match the added drain on the institution's resources, programs may become untenable. Additional costs are not only limited to instructional and support categories but may result from higher recruitment due to the need to replenish the student pool more often. Nevertheless, a growing number of colleges are adopting accelerated degree programs.

EXTERNAL DEGREE PROGRAMS

A second type of new degree program offers alternative time, space, and requirement options. The external degree allows students the opportunity to meet degree requirements with little or no obligation to be present on a traditional campus. The program may closely parallel existing internal degree programs, or it may have its own requirements. Some external programs utilize traditional classroom instruction and evaluation techniques; others are based on experiential learning and credit by examination. The common denominator among all these programs is that they provide new educational opportunities. As Davis (1973) notes:

> External degree programs assume that the chief
> barrier to learning is lack of opportunity.
> If one can be clear about educational objec-
> tives, provide adequate tutorial devices,

maintain proper incentives, and provide adequate feedback through frequent testing, students will make adequate progress toward earning an academic degree or some more limited goal [p. 11].

In his study The External Degree, Cyril Houle observes that the roots of the external degree concept in America can be found in the diversification of the curriculum through the elective system. The breakdown of the classical curriculum led to the development of a system of courses, credits, and degree requirements based on credit-hour and quality-point accumulations. The uniformity and compartmentalization of this system "allows for almost endless adaptation to various institutional forms and bodies of content [Houle, 1973, p. 4]." Two adaptations, part-time and transfer students, challenged the assumption that only full-time residential, uninterrupted study was valid. The first efforts at external programs were responses to the special needs of part-time students.

Historical precedents for the external degree can be found in the open universities of England and Japan as well as within American higher education. The external degree has historical links with the correspondence and extension work carried on for years by such institutions as the University of Oklahoma, the University of Texas, and Southern Illinois University. It is also a continuation of the extension movement begun in the 1890s by Columbia, Wisconsin, Brown, Indiana, and Illinois. A well-developed program of external studies was available at the University of Wisconsin at the turn of the century. By 1910 over 5,000 persons were taking university correspondence courses and there were extension centers throughout the state (Davis, 1973, p. 4).

It was not until 1961, however, that the University of Oklahoma offered the first truly national off-campus degree, the Bachelor of Liberal Studies. Students in the program studied where they lived, attending only brief on-campus seminars. In 1970 the New York State Education Department introduced the first degree-by-examination program in this country. The New York Regents' External Degree now offers at least seven different degrees. During the 1970s, external degree programs have been developed at scores of institutions, from Empire State College and Syracuse in New York to California State University, Dominguez Hills.

193

Houle discusses three categories of external degrees: extension, adult, and assessment. Extension degrees are based on the same program as an institution's internal degree but with courses offered in different locations. It is directed at nonresident students but makes no special effort to adapt to the clientele beyond minimal geographic flexibility. "The extension degree centers on the belief that a man or woman living in the community requires the same kind of program as the postadolescent living on the campus [Houle, 1973, p. 15]."

As the participation in extension programs increased, it became clear that the traditional internal degree, transplanted to a new geographic location, did not enjoy the same success it had on the home campus. Institutions began to modify extension requirements to meet the needs of the clientele they served. The result, "focused directly on the nature of the mature person and the lifestyle he or she follows [Houle, 1973, p. 15]," is an adult degree. It may be designed for adults in general or for a specific, undereducated group such as armed forces personnel or women returning to school. Often an adult degree is awarded in "General Studies" or "Liberal Arts," reflecting the increased freedom allowed students in response to their greater maturity and experience. Teaching methods may depend more heavily on independent study, reading courses, and other techniques that increase the options available to the student. Degree requirements may be altered individually to allow each student to take advantage of specific strengths or interests.

Roosevelt University offers an External Degree which is an extension of an existing internal program directed toward adult learners: the Bachelor of General Studies (BGS). Both programs are administered by the University's College of Continuing Education, which was created to meet the needs of adults. The Bachelor of General Studies is a formal degree program for mature students with little or no college experience. Requirements include an orientation seminar, introductory work, a concentration, Senior Seminars, and an internship in Urban Experience.

The Roosevelt University External Degree provides an opportunity for adults who cannot attend regular classes to complete the BGS program by meeting the requirements through independent study, which relies on specially prepared study guides to take the place of live instruction. In contrast to classroom courses, in which all students study the same material, external courses are divided into learning units or modules; students can select the content of their courses according to their choice of modules. Guides for a complete program of study are available in only two concentrations, but students may combine external modules with regular on-campus instruction for concentrations in other areas. Students may enter the program at any time and proceed through the independent study at their own pace.

The Metropolitan College of Saint Louis University also offers an external degree program for adult learners, but its program is based on traditional classroom experiences with an option for credit for prior experiential learning. Classes are held in the evenings and on weekends at seven college centers located throughout the metropolitan Saint Louis area. The academic year is made up of three twelve-week sessions with a shorter summer school session.

Students with at least one semester in the Metropolitan program may apply for credit for experiential learning. Through the Prior Learning Outcomes (PLO) program, credit can be earned for evaluation of work-related or other experiences in which learning has occurred. Credit may also be earned by examination through the College Level Examination Program. Credit granted through Metropolitan's Prior Learning Outcomes program, credit by examination, and transfer credit constitute the College's "parallel and equivalent" forms of recognition of advanced level knowledge and skills acquired outside Metropolitan College's classrooms. Because the College offers alternatives to classroom instruction and accepts transfer credit, many Metropolitan College students complete requirements for a bachelor degree in two or three years instead of the usual four.

As a community-oriented undergraduate college for persons over twenty-two years of age, Metropolitan College offers a variety of learning experiences. In addition to long-term, degree-oriented programs, the curriculum includes short-term programs leading to certificates in such diverse fields as credit management and gerontology, and noncredit courses in leisure as well as academic areas. Faculty for the College are drawn from the regular Saint Louis University faculty and from business, government, and professional associations.

The newest and most ambiguous category of

external degrees is the assessment degree. It is
based on the idea that

> . . . one or more of the traditional proced-
> ures of higher education . . . can be so modi-
> fied or separated from the others that the
> actual learning of the student, rather than
> his completion of formal requirements, can
> become the center of attention and the basis
> of awarding the degree [Houle, 1973, p. 90].

Of the traditional assessment procedures--admission,
teaching, evaluation, and certification and licen-
sure--the latter three are most frequently the subject of program design. The procedures are usually
based on either previous learning or specific competences. The most widely used assessment technique
is the College-Level Examination Program, although
many institutions also develop their own assessment
techniques.

The University of Alabama offers an external,
experiential degree. Although the program is
designed to provide an alternative method for pursuing the traditional B.A. or B.S. degree, it is
housed in a separate division: New College.
Participants must be at least twenty-two years old
and are drawn primarily from Alabama.

An on-campus orientation session is required
of all students in the Alabama program. The time
is used to explain the degree requirements and the
general nature of learning contracts and independent
study. The session also provides an opportunity to
assess the student's position and help students get
acquainted with the staff. Beyond the orientation
session, work is contracted for by the student, who
retains the major responsibility for learning. The
program requires a distribution of introductory
work in the humanities, social sciences, and
natural sciences; a Depth Study; and a final project. Demonstrated prior learning, transfer
credits, results of national tests such as CLEP,
independent study, out-of-class learning, correspondence study, weekend or evening seminars, and educational television courses may be applied toward the
attainment of the degree.

In 1972, Florida International University (FIU)
instituted an external degree program designed to
serve the needs of the whole state. It offers
individualized, upper division programs with an
emphasis on adult education and life-long learning.
The program is designed not only to provide

opportunity to students whose needs are not being met by other programs, but also to do so in a manner which is cost-effective relative to traditional programs.

The FIU External Degree Program is a self-directed, largely off-campus academic program. Students in the program earn baccalaureate degrees through a combination of credit for previous academic work and life experience, independent study, equivalency testing, and regular classroom courses at any college or university in the state. Together, the student and his faculty advisor, who is an expert in the student's chosen field of study, write an individualized program of study known as the educational contract.

The essential ingredient of the External Degree Program is the tutor-student relationship. Each faculty advisor assumes primary responsibility for the student's educational program, as outlined in the educational contract. This contract is a dual purpose instrument used both for assessing the present level of a given applicant's achievements and for outlining the program of study to be followed.

At the core of the educational contract is an educational project which may involve a major research paper, a number of independent study segments or courses, and field or work experiences. Many students in the program take some formal classroom work, although some take none. There are no formal curricular requirements in the External Degree Program.

Although the FIU program is administered by the School of Independent Studies, degrees for external students are granted by the traditional College of Arts and Sciences. This unique arrangement is designed to gain support for the external program among faculty and to minimize funding restrictions.

A final example of the new assessment degrees is the Humanities External Degree Program at California State University, Dominguez Hills. This institution now offers a fully accredited, worldwide, interdisciplinary program offering a bachelor (and master) degree waiving all attendance requirements.

At Dominguez Hills, those who enroll in the program are upper-division students who have already learned their basic study skills through two years of work at a community or junior college. In designing the program, the faculty abolished the traditional mode of teaching the humanities in favor of an interdisciplinary field of study with a degree awarded in the humanities rather than in specific subjects such as English, history, or literature. Each course examines topics from at least three of five humanities disciplines. The most noteworthy feature of the program is the absence of mandatory campus attendance for students. Unlike most external degree programs, which include periodic evaluations on campus or at "learning centers," the Dominguez program is built on the premise that mandatory campus attendance is not necessary.

The curricular concept underlying the Dominguez Hills program is referred to as "faculty-guided independent study." In the early stages of the program, all students in a course do the same assigned reading and writing; later on, students are allowed more freedom, carrying out individual study projects based on course topics.

To provide a learning framework, every student receives a packet or syllabus of study materials for each course. The packets include tape cassettes of lectures and seminars, reading lists, study guides, book reviews, and essay and study questions. Each course has its own study guide, which may be anywhere from 50 to 200 pages long. Instead of traditional examinations, students are graded on the basis of their essays on questions from the study guide. These papers usually range from two to twenty pages; a student will normally write over 100 research papers for the bachelor degree.

Originally designed for California residents, the Dominguez Hills program has already begun to attract students from all over the country. According to a recent article on the program, "An airman stationed in North Dakota, a teacher in California, a sculptor in Oklahoma, a sailor on a fleet cruise through the Pacific, and a military wife now living in the Azores are some of the 200 students currently enrolled [Hill, 1978, p. 20]." Barely three years old, the Humanities External Degree Program at Dominguez Hills has already established itself as a legitimate alternative to full-time, on-campus learning.

The primary advantage of external degree programs is the extension of higher educational opportunities to a clientele--particularly adult and part-time students--inadequately served by traditional programs. The importance of this advantage to a particular institution depends on its goals. To the extent that an institution views meeting the needs of nontraditional students as one of its functions, the development of an external program may be very desirable. Without solid support based on commitment rather than convenience, it is unlikely that an external degree will become a strong complement to existing programs.

As with all degree programs, costs can be a problem for external degrees. Tuition and charges must be designed to support specific student requirements. Especially among schools experimenting with new types of instruction, the problem of designing tuition charges is both difficult and critical to the survival of the program. The impact of the addition of an external degree on an institution depends on the care with which the program is launched. Like any expansion, success depends on providing a desired opportunity to potential consumers. Still, the evidence of recent efforts suggests that well-planned external programs can become strong, integral parts of their institutions.

STUDENT-DESIGNED PROGRAMS

The principal concern of proponents of programs for student-designed degrees is the need for student involvement in the critical stages of educational planning. Student-designed programs make the act of planning an integral part of the curriculum, often by requiring special seminars or tutorials on the problems of designing individual programs. Most student-designed degree programs, by definition, include student-designed majors (see chapter four). In addition to permitting freedom in the major, however, such degree programs recognize that students should also be permitted to decide what areas of breadth will best complement their area(s) of concentration.

Implementation of programs which increase student involvement in setting educational goals may be undertaken for several reasons. For example, an institution may be seeking to expand its service to its existing clientele by including student options in its major degree programs, perhaps on an institution-wide basis. The need to develop a curriculum which will draw traditional students in a tight market may also motivate the implementation of student-designed programs, although the market motivation may also lead an institution to develop programs which appeal to students not presently

199

served by the school, often adult students. A
third, and perhaps most interesting, reason for
adopting a student-designed program is its ability
to act as a sensitive mechanism to keep the university abreast of changes in student needs and
desires. The lack of restrictive structure in
student-designed programs makes them an ideal mechanism for adapting to the needs of a diverse student
body.

There are four problems which must be faced in
implementing any student-designed degree program.
The first is the need to develop a framework which
will provide some structure for student decisions
while not being prohibitively restrictive. Often
the guiding framework is expressed in terms of
general areas of knowledge or specific competences
required of the student, who is free to choose how
to meet the requirements and possibly how much
emphasis to place on various tasks.

The second problem to be faced is the need for
quality assurance. To maintain the credibility of
a student-designed program, both within and outside
the institution, there must be a regular mechanism
for review of all program plans. Students should
understand that the flexibility offered by the program must be matched by the responsibility to make
choices consonant with the goals of the program.
Paired with the need for the student to accept
responsibility is the need for the institution to
provide timely and meaningful support to the participants. Preenrollment interviews, strong faculty
advising and counseling support, and group work or
social sessions are examples of ways in which an
institution can provide an environment which
fosters student-designed efforts.

The last problem facing the designers of programs which rely on student choice is the economic
stress and ambiguity of the programs. Most programs
require a major investment of faculty and administrative time in counseling, support, and evaluation.
The diversity of the programs chosen by the students
and the fact that much of their work is often not
based on traditional course and credit units makes
the design of tuition charges quite complicated.
Determining the costs of the individual programs
and the overall support mechanisms, as well as
developing an equitable schedule of student fees,
are critical to the overall survival of the plan.

Options for student choice can take many forms.
Programs which have little supporting structure and
are embedded in existing degrees are often

alternatives designed for a small group of exceptional students. Many colleges offer honors programs which are thematically-oriented and not based on existing courses or credit requirements. Another minimum structure approach is to allow individual students to develop a degree program of their own. It is up to the student to develop the initiative and locate support sources. The only structure required of the university in this approach is a mechanism for evaluating and approving degree proposals. Often the student's program will rely on regular courses for a framework and for quality assurance, but in a pattern that is not possible under existing degree requirements.

At the other end of the structural continuum are those institutions which grant all or a majority of their degrees through student-designed programs. Reasons for the massive institutionalization of student choice include the desire for a more flexible means of evaluating students, for greater integration of the curriculum, and, of course, for greater student involvement. One advantage of institution-wide student-designed programs is that they provide an ongoing demand for support services which fosters the efficient and effective development of counseling, advising, and evaluation.

Manhattanville College requires each of its students to be involved in designing their undergraduate experience through the mechanism of a "portfolio." The latter is a repository for the student's study program and the various evaluation documents generated by the student's work. The portfolio is evaluated after four semesters and at the time of application for the degree.

Student input at Manhattanville is concentrated in the design of the study program. During his freshman year each student works with a faculty member, known as a "preceptor," who acts as his adviser and teaches a freshman course based in the professor's discipline. This course is intended to develop the student's research, reading, and writing skills. Under the guidance of the preceptor, each student designs a tentative plan for the four-year baccalaureate experience, including reasons for the choices the student has made. Structure is provided through general requirements that include work in a major field, significant work in a second field, exposure to a third field, and demonstration of the ability to relate the field of special interest to a wider intellectual human context. The

201

portfolio must also show examples of the student's best work which meets three specific competences: the ability to do independent work; mastery of the techniques of bibliography, research, and the method of inquiry; and evidence of critical insight. Manhattanville views the portfolio as "a means both to organize the learning process and to evaluate academic achievement [Manhattanville College Catalog, 1977-1978, p. 7]."

Midway between institutions offering informal options and those granting choices to all students are those colleges which provide a structured student-designed program for a relatively small number of students, often from a group not previously served by the college. These programs are based on the idea that there are students who are capable of taking on significant responsibility for their education and who cannot easily meet the time, space, and course requirements of existing programs.

Oklahoma City University (OCU) offers a Competency-Based Degree Program (CBDP) as "a distinctly different, academically effective, and fiscally efficient alternative to the traditional baccalaureate degree structure." The average age of CBDP students is thirty-eight, well above the average for students in OCU's traditional degree program. Consequently, the students are more likely to be married and 71 percent are employed full-time. Work and family demands make it unlikely that these students could participate in a traditional program.

The Competency-Based Degree Program differs from the traditional degree structure in that the criteria for awarding the degree are the achievement and demonstration of competence rather than the accumulation of a designated number of credit hours and specific courses. The CBDP uses a contract learning approach and allows for a high degree of individualization in both the learning outcomes achieved and the process by which the learning is achieved. As such, the CBDP requires a high degree of self-direction and self-discipline on the part of the student. Each student works with a faculty coordinator who assists him in planning and developing his program and Degree Contract. Additional faculty members are utilized as consultants for the planning, supervision, and assessment of learning contracts.

Each student, under the guidance of his Coordinator, writes a Degree Contract that includes: 1) the student's competences; 2) how the competences will be obtained; and 3) how the competences will be

verified and documented. The competences are organized into six Liberal Arts Competence Areas and
the Area of Concentration. The six Liberal Arts
Competence Areas comprise approximately 60 percent
of the student's degree program and the Area of
Concentration comprises 40 percent of the Degree
Contract. After completion of the Degree Contract,
the student devises one final learning project
called the Culminating Project.

A unique feature of the OCU program is the
CBDP Colloquium. It is a bimonthly meeting of all
CBDP students and is designed to perform two support
functions: to act as a problem-solving group and to
act as a support and social group. In addition, it
is also intended to act as an integration mechanism
for the liberal arts and to function as a community
of scholars.

The primary advantage of student-designed programs is their recognition of the individual's need
and ability to become involved in planning his
degree program. The act of designing the program
itself becomes a part of the educational experience
and represents an opportunity for student growth.
Student-designed programs are also an important
method of providing flexibility to students who cannot meet existing requirements or who want the
opportunity to study an area not offered. To the
extent that the options offered meet these needs,
student-designed programs are an attractive alternative for many students. Another advantage of
student-designed programs is their sensitivity to
change through the pattern of participant requests
which serve as automatic feedback for curricular
adjustment.

The major disadvantage of student-designed programs is their cost. Regardless of the format,
supporting this option draws heavily on institutional resources. In the most informal of programs,
faculty members may give extra attention to individual, exceptional students. As the burden of one-
to-one contact increases, however, the institution
faces the need to deal with the costs of the program
in terms of both revenues and expenditures. Still,
these cost problems are not insurmountable as a
wide variety of institutions--from large, public
universities like the University of Michigan to
small, private liberal arts colleges like Aquinas
College--have recently adopted student-designed
degree programs.

ORGANIZING PRINCIPLES AND STRUCTURAL VARIABLES

This chapter has presented examples of innovations in two types of structural variables: calendar modifications and new degree programs. It is important to reemphasize the relationship of these structural considerations to the choices made in other curricular areas. Viewing the curriculum as a system alerts the planner to the fact that maximum effectiveness can best be achieved if all component parts are compatible. This view allows us to understand that the choice of an organizing principle may lead to particular structure decisions. For example, student-designed programs, by including students in the educational planning process, are a natural vehicle for a curriculum which emphasizes student development. A program of this type would also suggest an emphasis on the contractual or student side of the Design of Program continuum (see figure 3).

Not only must the organizing principle, curricular emphases, and curricular structure match, but within each of these areas choices made by planners must recognize the interdependencies in the curriculum. As discussed earlier, Stephens College has adopted both an accelerated degree program and a modular calendar. Among the reasons for the calendar change was the need to provide greater access to courses for Three-Year students. Without the opportunity to enroll in more courses through the modular calendar, the freedom allowed by the new degree program might have led only to frustration.

The innovations described in this chapter are useful input for any curriculum planning process. Calendar and Degree Programs are curriculum areas which are often viewed as inflexible but are in fact quite amenable to change. Comprehensive curricular evaluation should include an assessment of these frequently overlooked components of the undergraduate program.

REFERENCES

Association for Innovation in Higher Education. Newsletter. St. Petersburg, Florida, 1974.

Davis, James R. "The Changing College Calendar." Journal of Higher Education, 43 (1972): 142-150.

Davis, James R. "The Walls Come Tumblin' Down:
    External Degrees and Experiential Education."
    Unpublished paper, 1973.
Earnest, Ernest. Academic Procession: An Informal
    History of the American College. Indianapolis,
    Indiana: Bobbs-Merrill, 1953.
Halliburton, David. "Curricular Design." In
    Arthur W. Chickering, David Halliburton,
    William H. Berquist, and Jack Lindquist,
    Developing the College Curriculum. Washington,
    D.C.: Council for the Advancement of Small
    Colleges, 1977: 35-50.
Hill, Martin. "A Nontraditional External Degree."
    Change, 10 (1978): 19-21.
Hofstadter, Richard, and Wilson Smith. American
    Higher Education: A Documentary History. Vol.
    I. Chicago: University of Chicago Press, 1961.
Houle, Cyril O. The External Degree. San
    Francisco: Jossey-Bass, 1973.
Manhattanville College Catalog, 1977-1978.
    Purchase, New York: Manhattanville College,
    1977.
Muskingum College: Prospectus. New Concord, Ohio:
    Muskingum College, 1976.
Research Report. The Third Group of 3-Year
    Baccalaureate Degree Students. Geneseo, New
    York: State University College of Arts and
    Sciences, Office of Institutional Research,
    1976.
Schmidt, George P. The Liberal Arts College. New
    Brunswick, New Jersey: Rutgers University
    Press, 1957.
Schultze, L. Walter. The 3-1-3 Experiment: First
    Annual Report. Fredonia, New York: State
    University of New York, 1973.
Schultze, L. Walter. The 3-1-3 Experiment: The
    Second Year. Fredonia, New York: State
    University of New York, 1975.
Stephens College: A Report Submitted to the North
    Central Association. Columbia, Missouri:
    Stephens College, 1977.
Veysey, Laurence R. The Emergence of the American
    University. Chicago: University of Chicago
    Press, 1965.

Epilogue

Curricular reform and innovation have become
central topics of discussion in American postsecondary education. Many of the nation's colleges and
universities, as well as the popular press, are
trumpeting the need for reevaluation of the formal
undergraduate experience. Harvard University,
which has often been a bellwether in the history of higher education, has just adopted a new
general education program--its first major revision
since 1945. Scores of other institutions--from
small, independent colleges to large, public
research universities--are now embarking on the
path of curricular evaluation.

This book is a guide for students, faculty,
administrators, and others involved in the reexamination of undergraduate education. Above all, it
is a survey of recent curricular developments, giving special attention to trends and innovations,
institutional examples of reform, and key issues in
undergraduate education. Combined with Appendix B,
which provides additional sources of information on
curricular innovation, the narrative should provide
readers with a grasp of the main developments in
the area.

But equally important, this book emphasizes the
importance of systemic curriculum planning as an
ongoing process. As I have repeatedly emphasized,
the curriculum can be fruitfully viewed as a system
wherein changes in one part of the undergraduate
program may have consequences for other parts.
While I have offered my own framework for planning
in chapter two, the reader is encouraged to modify
that framework or develop his own if he prefers an
alternative approach. What is most critical is the
development of a framework that is useful to those
involved in the planning process.

In closing, this book should not be viewed as
a plea either for or against innovation and reform
in American higher education. Institutional diversity, especially in the area of curriculum, is a
highly valued characteristic of American postsecondary education; it is a paradox that books discussing
innovation may unwittingly foster uniformity rather
than diversity. I hope that this book will not be
used as a blueprint for change but as a tool for
raising critical issues, identifying the kinds and
range of innovation in American higher education,
and encouraging systematic approaches to planning
the undergraduate program.

Appendix A:
Colleges and Universities
Referred to in the Text

Alverno College (Milwaukee, Wisconsin)
Amherst College (Amherst, Massachusetts)
Antioch College (Yellow Springs, Ohio)
Appalachian State University (Boone, North Carolina)
Aquinas College (Grand Rapids, Michigan)
Brigham Young University (Provo, Utah)
Brown University (Providence, Rhode Island)
California State University, Dominguez Hills
      (Dominguez Hills, California)
California State University, Fullerton (Fullerton,
      California)
Central Washington University (Ellensburg,
      Washington)
College of William and Mary (Williamsburg, Virginia)
College of Wooster (Wooster, Ohio)
Colorado College (Colorado Springs, Colorado)
Columbia University (New York, New York)
Emory and Henry College (Emory, Virginia)
Empire State College (Saratoga Springs, New York)
Evergreen State College (Olympia, Washington)
Florida International University (Miami, Florida)
Florida State University (Tallahassee, Florida)
Goddard College (Plainfield, Vermont)
Goshen College (Goshen, Indiana)
Harvard University (Cambridge, Massachusetts)
Haverford College (Haverford, Pennsylvania)
Indiana University (Bloomington, Indiana)
Juniata College (Huntingdon, Pennsylvania)
Manhattanville College (Purchase, New York)
Mars Hill College (Mars Hill, North Carolina)
Massachusetts Institute of Technology (Cambridge,
      Massachusetts)
Metropolitan State University (Minneapolis,
      Minnesota)
Michigan State University (East Lansing, Michigan)
Morningside College (Sioux City, Iowa)

Muskingum College (New Concord, Ohio)
Northeastern University (Boston, Massachusetts)
Oklahoma City University (Oklahoma City, Oklahoma)
Oregon State University (Corvallis, Oregon)
Ottawa University (Ottawa, Kansas)
Our Lady of the Lake University (San Antonio, Texas)
Prescott College (Prescott, Arizona)
Purdue University (Lafayette, Indiana)
Roosevelt University (Chicago, Illinois)
St. John's College (Annapolis, Maryland)
Saint Joseph's College (Rensselaer, Indiana)
Saint Louis University (St. Louis, Missouri)
San Francisco State University (San Francisco,
    California)
Seattle University (Seattle, Washington)
Southern Illinois University (Carbondale, Illinois)
Spring Arbor College (Spring Arbor, Michigan)
Stanford University (Stanford, California)
State University of New York, Binghamton
    (Binghamton, New York)
State University of New York, Brockport (Brockport,
    New York)
State University of New York, Fredonia (Fredonia,
    New York)
State University of New York, Geneseo (Geneseo, New
    York)
Stephens College (Columbia, Missouri)
Sterling College (Sterling, Kansas)
Sweet Briar College (Sweet Briar, Virginia)
Syracuse University (Syracuse, New York)
Trinity College (Hartford, Connecticut)
University of Alabama (University, Alabama)
University of California, Santa Cruz (Santa Cruz,
    California)
University of Cincinnati (Cincinnati, Ohio)
University of Denver (Denver, Colorado)
University of Evansville (Evansville, Indiana)
University of Illinois (Urbana, Illinois)
University of Kentucky (Lexington, Kentucky)
University of Oklahoma (Norman, Oklahoma)
University of Pennsylvania (Philadelphia,
    Pennsylvania)
University of Pittsburgh (Pittsburgh, Pennsylvania)
University of Texas (Austin, Texas)
University of Utah (Salt Lake City, Utah)
University of Wisconsin, Green Bay (Green Bay,
    Wisconsin)
University of Wisconsin, Madison (Madison, Wisconsin)
Warner Pacific College (Portland, Oregon)
Wheaton College (Wheaton, Illinois)
Yale University (New Haven, Connecticut)

Appendix B:
Major Organizational
Sources of Information
on Curricular Innovation

The following organizations are among those agencies, associations, information centers, and networks concerned with identifying and circulating information about innovation in undergraduate education.

American Association for Higher Education

AAHE members are often interested in trying new approaches and in making reforms happen; membership in the Association puts members in touch with these persons and their ideas. For instance, in conjunction with ERIC/Higher Education, AAHE publishes research reports on new programs, trends, and innovations in postsecondary education.

    For information:
        American Association for Higher Education
        One Dupont Circle
        Suite 780
        Washington, D.C. 20036

Association for Innovation in Higher Education

The Association for Innovation in Higher Education, formerly the 4-1-4 Conference, encourages innovation in higher education through cooperation and exchange of experiences utilizing workshops, meetings, seminars, and publications.

    For information:
        Association for Innovation in Higher
          Education
        Post Office Box 12560
        St. Petersburg, Florida 33733

Cooperative Education Research Center

The Cooperative Education Research Center attempts to respond to the informational needs of the cooperative education community. Among other

publications, the Clearinghouse on Cooperative
Education is an annotated bibliography on published
and unpublished papers on cooperative education.
In addition, the Research Center conducts an annual
survey of cooperative education programs in the
United States and Canada.

> For information:
> Cooperative Education Research Center
> Northeastern University
> Boston, Massachusetts 02115

Council for the Advancement of Experiential Learning

CAEL is an educational association for the purpose of fostering experiential learning and the
valid and reliable assessment of experiential learning outcomes. CAEL, originally known as the
Cooperative Assessment of Experiential Learning,
began as a research and development project involv-
ing the Educational Testing Service and a group of
colleges and universities. The Council now has a
current membership of some 300 institutions of
higher education. CAEL offers the most comprehensive set of materials available on experiential
learning. Their publications are directed to the
student learner as well as faculty and administrators.

> For information:
> CAEL
> American City Building
> Suite 208
> Columbia, Maryland 21044

ERIC Clearinghouse on Higher Education

The Office of Education has established sixteen
ERIC (Educational Resources Information Center)
clearinghouses which can provide useful background
information in the form of literature-based reviews
on issues in higher education. The Clearinghouse
on Higher Education directs its considerable
resources and products to serving the higher education community through the ERIC system in a variety
of ways. In addition to abstracting documents and
annotating journal articles for two monthly biblio-
graphic journals, Resources in Education and Current
Index to Journals in Education, the Clearinghouse
offers a computer search service of documents cited
in those journals. By contacting the Clearinghouse
with a search question, a computer-generated bibliography on the topic can be provided within a short
period of time.

For information:
          ERIC Clearinghouse on Higher Education
          One Dupont Circle
          Suite 630
          Washington, D.C.   20036

National Center for Public Service Internship Programs

The National Center was designated to dissemi-
nate information about nontraditional learning
opportunities to students of all ages. The
National Center serves as a resource center for
information about internships and fellowship opportunities for undergraduate and graduate students,
postgraduate students, and midcareer professionals.
          For information:
          National Center for Public Service
            Internship Programs
          1735 Eye Street N.W.
          Suite 601
          Washington, D.C.   20036

Society for Field Experience Education

The Society for Field Experience Education
(SFEE) serves as a forum and resource for persons
and institutions concerned with making off-campus,
field-based learning a significant component in
education. Through national conferences, task
forces reporting to the membership, and publications, the Society brings people, ideas, and
resources together.
          For information:
          Dr. Jane S. Permaul, Dean
          Experimental Education Programs
          UCLA
          Los Angeles, California 90024

Washington Center for Learning Alternatives

Started in 1975, the Washington Center for
Learning Alternatives (WCLA) is a nonprofit corpora-
tion designed to develop and administer programs
with components of experiential education in the
Washington, D.C. area. More than 200 colleges and
universities are now affiliated with the Washington
Center as a way of offering a wide variety of
internships for undergraduate and graduate credit.
Students' interests and abilities are matched
against a broad range of government agencies and
private organizations that have agreed to provide
supervised internships, eventually arriving at a
placement acceptable to both student and agency.

212

Because WCLA does not grant credit, each student
remains enrolled in his own college or university
and receives academic credit from that institution.
However, WCLA sends the institution advisory evaluations of each student's performance in both the
internship and a seminar.

For information:
    Washington Center for Learning
      Alternatives
    1705 DeSales, N.W.
    Washington, D.C. 20036